GREASY SIDE DOWN

A MILLION MILES ON MOTORCYCLES

GREASY SIDE DOWN

A MILLION MILES ON MOTORCYCLES

KENNETH (KEN) S. OBENSKI

ISBN: 978-1-956074-33-8 (Paperback Edition)
ISBN: 978-1-956074-34-5 (Hardcover Edition)
ISBN: 978-1-956074-32-1 (E-book Edition)

Book Ordering Information

Phone Number: 315 288-7939 ext. 1000 or 347-901-4920
Email: info@globalsummithouse.com
Global Summit House
www.globalsummithouse.com

Printed in the United States of America

DEDICATION

THIS is dedicated to my wife Cindy who does everything and encourages me when I want to do something that needs to be done that no one want to do.

Acknowledgment

I want to acknowledge the hundreds maybe thousands of people who crossed my path some to help me and some of whom presented me with a challenge. Without all those interactions I wouldn't be where I am today which happens to be a very good place.

CONTENTS

PART ONE

INTRODUCTION

MOTORCYCLE people are different. In Asia or Africa, it's mostly a matter of economy. Cheap bikes that get great gas mileage. India built the first practical diesel motorbike, (The US military copied it so they can have bikes that run on the same fuel as their trucks, tanks and helicopters.) Pictures circulate of a family of 5 on a moped. In America economy is seldom the main criterion. Cheap used cars are plentiful, reliable and easily serviced. Motorcycles, whether moped or *motorbago*, are fun. Easy to park, most of the time, except on steep hills where the one tire must touch the curb law conflicts with the stability on the kickstand. Motorcycles recall the free-wheeling spirit of the wild west, even in New York.

The fun takes many forms, there is the thrill of speed if you want it. Going 50mph in the open air feels like 200mph in a metal box. If you push the speed envelope, you can feel like a fighter pilot, with about the same risk too. Riders accept a level of risk that most people do not. Road rash is common and a few broken bones are accepted. Every activity has some risk. Couch potatoes get heart attacks. Motorcycle couriers in congested cities seem absolutely reckless to the people they pass, yet they get the rush packages through without crashing, or their service would not be viable. Motorcycle taxis are not unheard of, some include a cell phone connection for the glitterati rushing between openings and cocktail parties. Nothing decongest traffic like being about half as wide as a car with twice the acceleration.

Horseback was once considered first class travel! Faster than a wagon or carriage on unpaved roads, less likely to get stuck or robbed. Motorcycles fit that part of culture, true riders are exposed, but modern riding gear makes that a minor issue. A rider and

13

motorcycle seem to fit together like dressage where the horse seem to follow the riders will with no visible instruction. A man on a horse can go faster and farther that a man on foot. If he has access to fresh horses or another tank of gas a rider can go on for days. The control inputs are so subtle an observer could conclude the bike is autonomous.

Unlike a driver or passenger, a rider is part of the environment, when it rains, he gets wet, on the other hand he can smell the flowers, and the bakery treats, but also the diesel exhaust. On a bike small changes in the temperature of humidity are instantly apparent. Most motorcycles can go places many people would think require four-wheel drive, or a burro.

Then there is acceleration, nothing has the visceral stimulation of acceleration. Unlike other thrills, acceleration is felt in every cell of the body at the same time, every nerve is loaded. That is the thrill of roller coaster amusement park rides. The difference is that in the park ride the design of the ride determines the g level; on a bike the rider determines the g level, limited only by physics or nerve. Very few other surface vehicles can achieve one full g.

There is little that is as satisfying as winding a mountain road at ten tenths, or whatever the limit of your comfort calls for.

I'm just a little past halfway on the million miles, but the title flows better without the extra syllables. There are virtual miles that I have learned from other people's experience. It's taken me less than 50 years to accumulate over half, so it's still possible, although 1000-mile days on an island become repetitive. Even the "Big Island" of Hawaii is pretty small compared to North America, the perimeter highways add up to about 330 miles. With pathetically low speed limits. The default speed limit on county roads is 25 and it takes an act of the county council to change it anywhere. The highest we have is 60 on a road that would be posted 80 in western states. It is however quite an experience. Sea level to almost 14000 feet with a detour. Oops 4WD required above 9000 feet or down to Waipio valley, 35% grade 4WD again! You can see the wrecks, in the woods, of cars that could not handle it. I have seen ATVs go up and down, and suspect some dirt bikes. By the way, I do not consider anything with more than 2 wheels a motorcycle. They do not handle the same way. More about that later.

A trip around Hawaii Island is like a trip around the world. Desert, check; Rain Forest, check; Snow, check; Permafrost, check; Volcanoes, check; Jungle, check; Rolling grassland, check; Deep canyons, check; Waterfalls, check; Beaches, double check; Rocky rugged shorelines, check; Blowholes, check; Caves, check. One of the biggest books in my library is Hawaiian Geology. One Island with four National Parks: Hawaii Volcanoes, *Pu'uohu O Honaunau, Koloko Honokohau and Pu'ukohala Heiau.* Only Alaska, California and Utah have more; Utah is 20 times as big. We call it the world's most compact continent. We can have all four seasons at the same time. One of the wettest places on Earth and one of the driest are 6 miles apart. Hawaii county is a small town with very long streets. We have 200,000 people, same as Grand Prairie Texas. Only 45 people per square mile, like Oklahoma. On the other hand, every natural disaster is possible here. As I write this page, we are sheltering in place from COVID.

PROLOGUE

I'M an unlikely product of an improbable marriage. Meeting my parents was like discovering Eric Sevareid was married to Carol Channing, or Barak Obama to Cindy Lauper. First, my Mother was a serious swimmer from an old world conservative Jewish family. Her parents were born in Russia. Her Dad had a medal from the Russia Japanese war. Her brothers were born in Russia, England, America and an immigrant ship. My Dad was born to a Polish family, raised as a Catholic sent to parochial schools. Poland was part of Russia when they emigrated. My parents lives crossed in a strange way. Mom was a champion swimmer, she competed with men. She was in a diving competition, at 17, when she felt a snap in her spine. She was diagnosed with an unnamed degenerative condition and never expected to walk again, let alone have children. A brash young surgeon, I heard his name as MacPhedron (sp), said let me try and had her moved to Germantown Hospital. She wore a full body cast for over 3 years while being injected with almost every drug known to man in 1932. She was very close to her Father who died of tuberculosis, maybe related. I believe he was 58.

Parochial school required pupils to attend mass every Sunday. Dad did not, so he got a whipping every Monday. He said the whipping did not hurt as much as sitting through the mass so he never reformed. He went to Wissahickon Park instead. He was an excellent student and even without the benefit of mass he was elected valedictorian. In those days there was only one valedictorian to a class. Unfortunately, he contracted pneumonia and was unable to attend his own graduation. Instead, he was sent to Germantown Hospital. There was no real treatment for pneumonia in those days, 1932. The patient was put in an oxygen tent and prayed for. The first antibiotic, penicillin did not come along until 1942. His family prepared for his funeral. The men bought black ties. The parish priest came to the hospital and gave him the last rites. As you might have suspected by now, he didn't die. When it was obvious that he was going to live the priest visited him and said, "Well John now that God has spared you; I expect we will be seeing you in church."

Pop told him "As far as you are concerned, I'm dead." And he never went to church again, except funerals and weddings. We call it the F&W church. Those black ties, he wore them to the funerals of his younger brother who died of pneumonia and his father, when I was 8. He was the oldest son and the last to pass, although he had been a sickly child.

Pop was hospitalized for a long time. After a while they let him roam the hospital and encouraged him to visit the solarium where he could focus the sun-shine into his throat to kill the infection. He met a young redhead there who was also a long-term patient. They spent a lot of time together having little else to do. TV wasn't invented yet either. His voice remained soft. The staff commented that he couldn't walk and she couldn't walk. I guess that passed for coffee break philosophy.

When Mom told her Father, about John she expected a lot of resistance for dating outside the faith, but her Father whom I never got to meet just said "Better a good Polack than a bad Jew." Fortunately, there was no religious stress between my parents.

Pop said, "I don't care what you do, I just want Christmas." And he meant the fun part. We sort of celebrated Jewish holidays, I was Bar Mitzvah, we had a menorah and a Christmas tree – seasonal shrub I named it and stuff like that with the whole Obenski/Schuman clan. Mom joined a Reform Synagogue and Pop even went with her on some holidays, but he just attended. His mind worked on something else constantly anywhere. Ultimately his silence spoke louder than her praying and I became a devout agnostic. Many years later his mother told us that she didn't know what to do one Sunday so she went to mass and got bored quickly and left early. I guess it runs in the family.

Pop aspired to be an auto mechanic but Jewish Mom had to have a white-collar husband. She pushed him to try something else. Pop was good at drafting and had little trouble getting hired as a draughtsman at Baldwin Locomotive Works. Within six weeks was a supervisor. He moved up quickly and escaped WWII because by the time his number came-up he had become an engineer designing tracking and elevating mechanisms for coast defense 8-inch guns. In case you are unfamiliar 8-inch is the diameter of the bullet. That makes the barrel over 30 feet long. The Military seemed to agree that designing big guns was more important than carrying a little one. He was deferred until '44 when they decided his one blind eye disqualified him permanently from service. His brothers served. He engineered the Jaws of Life®.

Mom was a pioneer in her own way, she insisted on natural, unmedicated, childbirth in the age of knock 'em out drag 'em out obstetrics, and insisted on breast feeding in the age of "modern way" formula feeding. Unfortunately, her mother was so ill that we had no real relationship except with her extended family.

I was born in 1944, ahead of the baby boom and was only 5 when I started first grade. No kindergarten in those days. I was always the youngest, smallest and athletically most ungifted in all my classes. I might have been the first Jew in the school. Most people's muscle tissue is a mix of slow twitch and fast twitch. Great athletes have mostly fast twitch muscles and that is why they can jump so high, hit so hard etc. I think mine are all slow twitch. I can barely hit a slow pitch softball. I did learn, too late for high school athletics, that I had a talent that could have been valuable in football. I could keep moving the ball forward even after several players piled on.

Denver and Rio Grande antique narrow-gauge locomotive

Trains were also in my blood. In addition to Pop's experience at Baldwin, my Grandfather took me to Wayne Junction to watch the locomotives up close, and Uncle Joe worked as a railway brakeman for a year. Pop built a magnificent train platform for us every Christmas until one year he was running late and I started finishing wiring his work. That was a huge mistake, once he saw what I could do, though not as well, he lost the motivation. I have started quite a few layouts, but have yet to get to the point that anyone would consider them finished. Even if one is finished, it never is. Hundreds of models though, most from kits, but a few scratch-built some kit-bashed, that is seriously modified.

Another peculiar factor is how I came to be an author. I enjoy the creativity of writing, but absolutely detest the physical act of writing. This stems from my third-grade teacher who traumatized the entire class, but me especially. On the first day she assigned more homework that could possibly be completed. I was up 'til eleven, then up again at 5AM, but still did not finish. All the parents complained and she reduced the assignments to about 4 hours a night, I was seven. Asking to use the pencil sharpener was treated like a high crime or misdemeanor and subjected the requester to suspicion and intense scrutiny. Her stare could not have been more penetrating if she was looking over a shotgun. That made me so nervous I broke my pencil. The result was that I wrote half the assignments holding a broken off pencil point between my thumb and forefinger. My handwriting is abominable. Maybe that is why I had so much trouble with punctuation. My school district did not teach boys typing (except one week) so I did not learn that essential skill. Only the invention of the word processor, with spell and grammar check, made writing something I could really do on my own. I have learned more about punctuation from Word, than school.

We had boats so I started learning a little about driving quite young, maybe 10, and I had a bicycle from about the age of 5. My first was a 20-inch "girls" bike with a step through frame, but at least it did not have training wheels. Next bike my first real bike was a J C Higgins 24- inch balloon tires with a fake gas tank to make it look vaguely like a motorcycle. There was a horn in the fake gas tank. Once I had that, I did some real riding outside the neighborhood. I even got to the point with that of riding it almost a half mile to a girl's house, to impress her. She wasn't.

Finally, at 11, I got an "English Racer," that is a bike with narrower tires and a gear shift. Three speeds! Hand operated brakes with the rear on the right and front left. Mine was actually made in England, a Raleigh with an enclosed chain and a generator in the front hub for the lights.

Bicycles were the path to independence. Took me where I felt I needed to go until I got a motor. At 12 I had my first cycle crash. Racing to the corner store with neighbor Johnny. He turned in front of me then suddenly stopped. I crashed into him and flew over the handlebars landing on my left arm. He said "Why'd y' do it Ken?" I noticed I had an extra wrist and said "I think my arm's broken." I walked home, a half a block. Pop saw me coming and could see something was wrong. He took me to the local hospital. They kept me overnight after giving me enough morphine for me to experience withdrawal at bedtime. It was easy to see how one could become addicted to morphine it creates a feeling of over-all well-being.

Although we lived in the 'burb that is Hatboro PA, across the street was Warminster, Bucks County mostly vacant land. We belonged to some clubs where Pop let me drive on private property before I was quite legal. As I approached driving age my bicycle excursions got way beyond the neighborhood. Not that it was anything heroic, but 20-25 miles round trip in a day. I learned to slipstream a truck to go much faster than I could pedal alone.

A word about Hatboro, we actually lived ten feet from it in a township called Upper Moreland. Hatboro was a borough which is the title Pennsylvania gives to small municipalities. Townships are larger and more rural. Most of Pennsylvania is townships, which may contain what looks like a town, or more than one, sort of like a mini county. Upper Moreland and Hatboro were high school football rivals.

Our neighborhood was a peculiar political extension of Upper Moreland Township that enclosed the borough of Hatboro on three sides. It took 15 minutes from our house to downtown Hatboro, on foot, half that on a bike. That was where I had my second crash. Riding on the sidewalk, an indecisive young woman stepped the wrong way, I swerved to miss her and hit a utility pole. The woman was un-harmed as was the pole. I saw stars but other than that seemed to have no ill effect. Nobody thought of helmets in those days.

I enrolled in Penn State at Ogontz Campus, a commuter school, where I lasted one term (trimester, 10 weeks). Goofed off a while, worked part time in the neighborhood grocery, then got work as a surveyor's entry level assistant, apprentice, Rod-and-Chain Man. That's the guy who holds the stupid end of the tape, or balances the rod, a giant ruler, so the Instrument Man can read the vertical measurement that is level with his scope, or any other mundane task.

My First A Whizz

My first "motorcycle" was a Whizzer moped my Dad bought for $15; (gas was $0.13 a gallon). It was a motorcycle in that it had a motor, and two wheels. It also had pedals which in those days was the definition of a moped unlike the current definitions of moped that usually specify an engine of less than 50 ccs and do not always require pedals. Honda made its name with the Honda 50 motorcycle. The Whizzer had a 175cc flathead lawn mower type engine that probably made 3 horsepower. The only brand on the basic bike was B F Goodrich, apparently it was a tire store, balloon tire cruiser. Whizzer made the bolt on kit for the customer to motorize it at home. It had a rear coaster brake, and I vaguely remember a front brake lever, and an undersized hub brake. It had a V-belt drive with a lever operated belt tension release for a clutch.

The starting procedure was: open the compression release, put on the choke, pull in the clutch lever, pedal like crazy; then release the clutch, close the compression release and continue pedaling until you felt a push. When it settled down, open the choke.

It had no instruments, so I have no idea how much I rode it or how fast but I did ride it to work about 20 miles each way all one summer. It was not very fast, but downhill it did once keep up with traffic in a 45mph zone, on ten-year-old bicycle tires! I took it off road too. At least when it got stuck it wasn't very heavy, compared to a Harley. My memories fade after that; it was 1963. I remember a hysterical lecture from my mother that "You are a nice Jewish boy you should not be seen riding a motorcycle shirtless."

The last memory I have of the Whizzer is that the head gasket blew out and I had to pedal home, not far but it exhausted me. The clutch lever did not uncouple the engine well but the compression release helped. The Whizzer engine was very simple air cooled one-cylinder flat head. The valves and exhaust ports were all in the block. Removing the cylinder head was just 4 bolts. I could not get Whizzer parts, so I cut a new head gasket from some asbestos sheet made for a wood stove. It did not run well after that. Single cylinders run a bit rough, but when they are that small it's not too bad. We call bigger singles thumpers, and describe the engine idle as thud, thud.

My younger brother Mike wanted a motorcycle too. As soon as he turned 15, he started looking at Harleys but one visit to the dealer convinced him to wait. He was still pretty small then and he could not safely get a 600-pound Harley off the side-stand (kickstand). Not easily discouraged though, he found and bought a 1946 Harley Servicar® Tricycle, (aka trike), complete with suicide clutch and tow-bar hitch. The suicide clutch, or more accurately suicide shifter, was a feature of many early motorcycles before the modern foot shift that is so easy one learns to shift automatically. The suicide shift was a big lever on the left side, like you might find on a tractor. It had 3 forward gears plus neutral and reverse all in a line. To shift you had to let go of the left handle bar and while steering with one hand depress the heavy clutch pedal with your left foot and simultaneously wrestle the shifter to the next gear, then release the clutch. The positions were in one staggered line, not H pattern like a car. There were stops at some positions so you could feel where the lever was. It took physical strength and a lot of coordination to do that and go straight, thus the nickname.

I suppose I should describe the modern shifter for non-riders. There is a pedal on the left side near the left foot-peg, or foot-board if it's a Harley. The clutch lever is on the left handlebar and with a modern wet multi-plate clutch easy to pull in. Squeeze the clutch lever toward the handlebar, pull the foot lever up or down with your left toes to change to the next gear. Usually up for up, down for down, with neutral between 1 and 2. That makes it one click closer when you stop. Some bikes can go from high back to 1 by clicking up one more time. Oh, some bikes used to have the shifter on the right, opposite of the majority. Some had the clutch on the right and front brake on the left. Indian had the throttle on the left of police bikes so an officer could ride and shoot. Fortunately, by the time I got into motorcycles the main control locations were standardized. Clutch and gear-shift on the left. Throttle and both brakes on the right. Front brake on the right handlebars, opposite of a bicycle, foot brake for the rear. Some had an extension to the shift lever to allow upshifting with the heel, or if you were sitting far back toe- shift upside down with that extension. Some new models have the front and rear brakes integrated so that the foot pedal also applies the front brake. ABS is available too. Motor-scooters have their own control layout with an awkward, to me, shifter and clutch on the left grip. Squeeze the clutch, then rotate the assembly to the next notch and release, some are automatic. The turn signal is still an orphan, as each manufacturer does it their own way. Most have three-way switch on the left grip

Riding a trike sounds safer than a motorcycle, but motorcycles lean in a turn so you only feel the centrifugal force (centripetal acceleration if you are a physicist) holding you to the seat. I won't get into the argument of centrifugal force versus centripetal acceleration. Either term amounts to the same thing. A trike stands up, actually leans a little the wrong way and it feels like it's trying to throw you off, part of the reason 3-wheel ATVs are no longer manufactured. Imagine driving a stick shift car sitting on the roof. The steering is simple enough, but the tricycle arrangement is inherently unstable at speed. Without going into the physics, it wants to turn over, remember Laugh In? Two in front and one behind is much more stable, especially while decelerating in a turn. Another reason I don't consider a trike a motorcycle.

The Harley engine is a V twin, a shape that fits conveniently into a bicycle style "diamond" frame. Both connecting rods are on the same crankpin. Imagine a bicycle with both pedals not quite opposite one another either. When one is at the top, 12 o'clock the other is not at 6, but 2. The engine is hard to balance well because the firing impulses are unevenly spaced (about 412 degrees, 308 decrees) and the crankshaft cannot be completely balanced. It is basically, a seven-cylinder radial engine with five cylinders absent. The exhaust sound is often described as potato, potato. The engine is sometimes called a Milwaukee Vibrator, but many people find it soothing.

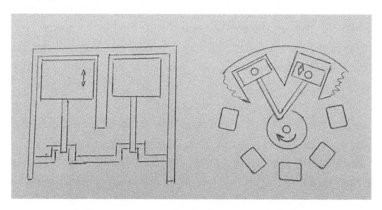

Traditional inline twin Cylinder - Vtwin / Radial

The Servicar® had a tow-bar and clamp on bumper hitch to make it possible for a mechanic to ride the trike to a customer's location and drive the customer's car to the shop towing the trike behind. Bumpers in those day were quite distinct from the car body with top and bottom edges exposed. Few people in those days had more than one car. The Servicar had a trunk to carry some basic tools to get the customers car running. The original sheet metal body was hopelessly rusted out, but with Dad's help we build a pretty cool looking pickup bed for it out of plywood and steel tubing.

Mike traded the whizzer for a 250 cc Indian® that he never got running in spite of having the magneto rebuilt. Mike also bought a MotoGuzzi® 250 twin with the transmission in a basket. There was at least one part missing and we never solved that puzzle.

There was a Triumph® shop behind my Dad's office, so he got to know the people there. One of them was trying out his new motorcycle riding past his motorcycle shop at about 50. He was distracted and must have forgotten it was a dead-end street. The bike crashed through a concrete block wall and the only mystery was why he lived long enough to get to the hospital, just long enough, but no more. Motorcycles are safe as long as you remember they're dangerous.

Career wise I was going nowhere, so I sold my MG sedan and joined the Army. They "guaranteed" my MOS would be Topographic Surveyor, consistent with my experience. I went to Basic Training at Ft Jackson SC. Just when I got to know my group, they cut off everyone's hair and identity. We had leave for Christmas then returned for a week before being sent to my Advanced Individual Training as a Topographic Surveyor at Fort Belvoir. I got orders to Korea, just in time to avoid being sent to Vietnam.

I did not have a bike at the time, but there are still stories. Our training platoon was 30 army privates and one Captain from the Thai Army. Pade Aimwonga and I became good friends, but of course he did not bunk with the rest of us. I maintained a pen pal relationship with him for another year. The topographic surveyor program was more like college than army except we slept 40 to room and no coeds. Strict lights out policy in the barracks meant studying in the latrine (toilet). We nicknamed our platoon the Shithouse Scholars of Company B.

Mostly we were well behaved but one night I came back to our barracks room on the second floor of an impressive building that from the outside looked like a dorm. There was chaos going on as those in the room had been short sheeting those absent. The pranks were becoming more creative until somebody said "What about Woody?" There were a lot of bizarre suggestions until I said.

"The thing that would bother him the most would be to be left out." and so he was. He came into the midst of the chaos and spent ten minutes trying to figure out what the prank on his bunk was. When he realized he had been left out he nearly cried.

The following night my bunkmate 'Fazz' and I had passes. We

were pretty sure our bunk would be the object of the continuation so we planned our response. Lights out was 2000. Therefore, everyone would be in bed asleep by 2300. Our passes were good until midnight, so we checked in at 2355 and went upstairs. We agreed that no matter how we found our bunk it would be the funniest thing we ever saw and would wake up every single other occupant of the room and tell them. The entire bunk was upside down, but neatly made up. We carried out our plan and got even.

A Dream

I spent a delightful year, 1965, in Korea, technically as a Topographic Surveyor, but rebranded as an Atomic Demolition Specialist by a Company Commander who felt that would increase his prestige. I was mostly an idler courtesy of the US Army. I think I spent less than 10 days of 13 months doing anything useful, and less than two days as a topographic surveyor. We would often take a coffee break and disappear for hours to the PX or a warehouse where we were expected to do something useful like polish the shovels every day. The KATUSAs, Korean Augmentation To US Army, polished their shovels so much they wore holes in them.

One of the things I learned about the Army was that they officially wanted us better educated and almost always gave me permission to go to the library. Korea was said to be the Army's best kept secret. Military pay went a long way in the Korean economy and PX but that's another book. Like many GIs, I had had a *Yobo*, sort of contract wife named Hwang Chung Hi. We had good times including trips to parks, monuments and the National Fair. The only thing I remember about the fair was an exhibit of semi diesel fishing boat engines. They came in 1,2,3,5,6, or 7 cylinders. Four is bad luck in the orient and nobody is more superstitious than fishermen. There were a lot of flowers and praise of the Korean alphabet Hangul that unlike other Asian languages was adaptable to a typewriter. The birthday of the inventor of the Hagul typewriter was a national holiday.

Chung Hi hoped I would marry her and take her to the land of the big PX, but my feelings did not go that deep. She was smarter than most business girls in that she opened a savings account. The

29

account sort of worked like a Christmas Club account here but every month the installment was decreased by the accumulated interest to encourage depositors to keep up. She bought a bookstore and married a Korean man willing to ignore her past! In the process I learned enough Korean language to carry on a simple conversation as long as people who knew me limited the topics. I even helped *Chung Hi's* landlady's kids with some homework.

My buddy Clem had a Korean girlfriend also named *Chung Hee*. (Different spelling in transliteration) Same as my Yobo. She was never a business girl; she was a charming hostess at an upscale OB beer hall where the local businessmen relaxed. OB was the preferred brand of Korean beer. Clem got court marshaled for staying overnight with her. He volunteered for Vietnam, and after he got out of the Army went back and married her. They are still together. We make contact about every ten years.

When we ordered a beer in Korea, we insisted on having the cap on. Otherwise they would serve you Crown, that taste worse than it looked, with the label washed off.

The war artillery destroyed all the trees in South Korea. To reforest they passed a law that made it illegal to cut down a tree. Instead, people broke off branches for firewood constantly and the trees did not grow.

Soldiers are great pranksters. If I asked a Korean soldier how to say something, I would then ask a different one, If I say this… what does it mean?

I decided that on my way home I would cross the continent on a motorcycle. At the library I researched things to see and mapped out my route. Unbelievably to me there was a part of California with no East West highways for over 200 miles. I figured I just needed to get to Cali and get better maps.

My parents agreed to loan me the price if I agreed not to camp. Mothers worry and there was an epidemic of rabid skunks that year. An army buddy, we called Rod gave me a place to stay at his parent's home in San Leandro, California for a few days and took me around to motorcycle dealers. Conventional wisdom was to get a bike of at least 250 ccs for such an undertaking. The best value I found was a Honda 300 Dream for $800. (Gas was about $0.30).

When I made the deal I wanted to add luggage. I chose the less expensive of two options, not realizing it was a single tail trunk instead of two saddlebags. It did protect my camera and that was important. When I picked up the bike they offered to teach me; that sounded good. We put the bike on the center stand, the one that lifts the rear wheel, and I got on. I started the engine shifted gears with my toe, and was told I knew enough, bye. More about that later.

My '66 Honda Dream 300

I learned by doing, and learned a lot. Riding a motorcycle is estimated to be five times as hard to learn as learning to drive a car. The first day on a new bike is about 60 times as dangerous as the hundredth day. (Hurt Report) I think that's why the dealer wants you off his lot ASAP.

Maybe they just wanted to see if I knew not to upshift with the heel shifter, not that it matters. I suppose the heel shifter could break something. They sold me a helmet I wanted, and recommended a bubble shield that I did not think I would need. I did, the first swarm of insects made me a believer. There is an old riddle: How do you tell a happy motorcyclist? By the bugs on his teeth. A swarm of gnats at 50mph feels like being sand blasted.

I had my Army duffel bag with 66 pounds of military clothing to deal with and orders to report to Fort Bragg, North Carolina. Fortunately, postal regulations allowed service members to mail their duffel bag issue with no weight restriction as long as it's from or to a military address so I did not have to deal with that. I packed the rest of my wardrobe in a gym bag bungeed to the seat and took off. I found new pair of sturdy Levi Straus button-fly jeans at a farm worker supply store for $3.33. Funny what one remembers.

Pacific to Atlantic was the goal so the first stop was to be the left coast. The owners- manual, quaintly written in Tokyo High School English, admonished me to "Use only high- quality fuel as furnished at reliable petrol stands." and not to exceed 35mph for the first 500 miles. Shortly found myself on the narrow two-lane San Mateo Bridge and discovered the speed limit was 50. With an 80,000-pound semi-truck tailgating me, I pushed it up to 40.

The exact route escapes me, but I remember cresting a hill and seeing a beautiful shore line with palm trees and neatly maintained suburban houses. I know palms are not really trees, but that's what people call them. Rode north along the coast and over the Golden Gate to Sausalito. There is an overlook on the north end of the bridge from which I could see Alcatraz and San Francisco. I did not get to visit Alcatraz until 50 years later. Sausalito was quaint and I remember seeing houseboats that looked like they were built on old lifeboat hulls and never moved. I wondered where the sewage went, but suspect I would not like the answer.

California was like a new country to me. Somewhere near Sacramento I recall a used house lot. Like a used car lot but with houses on blocks ready to be moved to the buyer's lot like a piece of furniture. In Pennsylvania where I grew up houses stayed put a couple of hundred years. I was fascinated by Central Valley farmland flat as a pool table and farm machinery the size of naval vessels. Where I grew up a really big farm was 300 acres. In the West they measure land in sections not acres. One section is 640 acres. A starter homestead was ¼ section. The Caterpillar tractor was invented by a California farmer to avoid the heavy early steam tractors sinking in soft mud. Although the Beach Boys California Girls ran in my head, I did not see any that impressed me; until I saw my first mini skirt. In early 1965 when I went over the dress code almost everywhere had been "skirts to cover the knee" suddenly 3,4,5 inches above the knee was common. Within a year the knee became an irrelevant reference. One inch shorter for every ten degrees above 70 was the rule of thumb at UA Phoenix where 130 degrees is not uncommon. They did not specify from where.

My next goal was Yosemite Park. Riding over the Coast Range Mountains I realized that when a motorcycle turns on the highway, there is almost zero movement of the handlebars, and it might even be the opposite of what you expect. Back when I was limited to a bicycle, I had had a scary experience coasting down a steep hill behind my highschool. More later. Leaning into the turn worked and the day was saved. Since then, I have learned a lot about motorcycle handling and counter-steering. In fact, I wrote books about it. (Lawyers and Judges Publishing) If you think you can ride a motorcycle, because you think you know how to ride a bicycle, you may be in for a surprise, or even a crash.

To turn a motorcycle abruptly, push on one handlebar, and that is the way the bike will lean. We call this counter-steering. The bars seldom actually move a noticeable amount. The bike will turn the way it leans until the bars are pushed the other way. Learning this skill goes a long way to surviving on a motorcycle. Even more deliberate control can be had by pulling the outside handgrip as one push the handgrip on the inside causing an abrupt change in lean angle. When the bike is at the correct lean angle force it back. Emergency maneuvers can be executed very quickly. Emergency counter-steering is the most important part of the motorcycle safety course according to many instructors. I have made videos to demonstrate this both in court and for education. On a video I demonstrated that it is possible to make a complete 12-foot lane change at 60mph in 1.3 seconds. I wanted to instrument a bike and see if the handlebar movement was even measurable, but never figured out how to measure such a tiny movement.

Winding mountain roads are where riding a motorcycle is a wonderful experience. Wonderful, until you have just switched the gas tank to reserve for the first time and you have no idea how much gas that is or where the next reliable petrol stand might be. I started shutting the engine off and coasting unless I was climbing. One huge advantage of touring by motorcycle is you do not need an official *scenic lookout* to pull over and look, most of the time the shoulder is 2 or 3 motorcycles wide. I did find brand name gas ($0.40) before running out and did not worry if Chevron qualified as a reliable petrol stand by Honda's definition.

I arrived at Yosemite area by the Big Stump entrance. The biggest tree I had ever seen, broken off at about 200 feet tall!

I had hoped to continue east from there, but learned to my amazement that the maps I had access to in Korea were right. I rode toward Tuolumne pass but it was closed until the snow melts, in July, maybe. Snowdrifts in the Sierra Nevada can be 200 feet deep! I enjoyed lunch in a bar in a tent that felt like it was 1880. Surrounded by people dressed like they might be prospectors. You cannot cross the Sierras between Donner Pass and Kernville, over 200 miles, except in the late summer, it was only April. So I headed south. Descending from Yosemite Park I learned a lot about braking a motorcycle. Don't brake hard on a curve; brake in a straight line, then turn; On long downgrades alternate front and rear brakes as needed to let them cool. This was before disc brakes.

Roads like this make motorcycles fun, or scary

I stopped for lunch at an attractive place called Snow Line Lodge. Attractive except for the 3x5 cards taped all over the interior. The cards all had a very similar message "We do not have (whatever anyone ever asked for) at Snow Line Lodge". I thought that was a pretty poor business plan. If you wanted a paper-clip, how would you know which card to read.

I promised my Mother I would call every night. A motel I stopped in was in Squaw Valley California, the original one, not the Winter Olympic imposter. Lodgings were proportionately less expensive, I think. In those days, no pool, TV, phone or minibar. The Post Office next door to the motel was in a shed about 8 feet square. When I asked about a pay telephone, I was given directions to the nearest one about ten miles. She did not get a call that night.

General Sherman Tree, I'm a dot at the bottom

I had my first Coors beer. After a year of Korean Beer it was refreshing, but now I agree it's like having sex in a canoe, f... near water.

General Sherman Tree, I'm a dot at the bottom I wanted to see the world's largest tree, the General Sherman. In the parking lot I handed my new, $100 at the PX in Korea, $300 retail, 35mm camera to another man with a Honda. I walked forever to the tree, starting to wonder if that was wise. When I got back, it seemed like an hour later, he handed my camera back". I guess you do meet the nicest people on a Honda, or did then. Months later I got to look at the picture I was just a dot at the base, the tree is over 300 feet tall. Funny thing about words. Tall is a Gaelic word that originally meant fast. Tall ships meant fast ships. The fast ships all had masts that reached to the sky, so the word took on a new meaning. Here is the mystery, does tall have a synonym? What English word did it replace? I can't think of one. Neither high, long or lofty works.

You may meet the nicest people on a Honda, but you meet the strangest people in the Army. Just in the 161 Engineering company which was half KATUSA. One that we called Lip named for his hare-lip was a lifer Specialist E5. I forget his real name and his specialty. He pitched for the company low pitch softball team and had a fastball that looked like it was shot out of a rifle, absolutely flat trajectory that would never rise above 18 inches, yet never miss the strike zone. Head was his best buddy, nick-named for his large peanut shaped head.

Another strange thing I learned about 1965 California. The towns can be so far apart that there is only one road, and it's a 4-lane freeway with 75mph traffic. As fast as I could go, it really felt fast after the Whizzer and Army trucks. California freeways taught me to be leery of rain grooves. The narrow motorcycle tires tend to follow the grooves instead of the path the rider wants, resulting is an unsettling zig zag as the tire tread wanders in the groove. The tire manufacturers have since then learned to take that into consideration in tread design. No more center rib.

Crossing the Sierras, I realized how futile invading America from the West coast would be. First of all the beaches are mostly small and rocky. The continental shelf drops off really fast. No shallow water for an artificial harbor like Mulberry. No significant islands to launch attack from. Many beaches are backed up with cliffs, then bays. The defenders could lob artillery onto any landers from miles inland. Then there is the coast range with just a few passes, a shotgun in every farm house and Admiral Yamamoto is said to have feared a rifle behind every blade of grass. Then invaders would come to the Sierras with narrow passes three hundred miles apart. The passes are 50 miles of ten percent grade to 7000-foot saddles. In between the ridges are, 10,000 to 14,000 feet. It took the USA 50 years to settle the west coast states. Most of the traffic went by sea, 13,000 miles around Cape Horn until after the Civil War.

The way east went through Kernville and Death Valley. Death Valley sounds ominous, but it was a paved road so how bad can it be? I saw a dead burro beside the road and decided to take a photo. When I pulled off the road onto the soft shoulder, I dropped the bike for the first time. Being a novice, I also got my leg pinned under it. An older couple where there, but instead of offering help, they just drove off. I guess they did not know you meet the nicest people under a Honda Pinned to the ground in Death Valley, how bad can it be? As you might have figured out by now, I did not die there. That bike just was not really all that heavy and with a little effort I pulled my leg out, didn't even tear the Levis. I photographed the bloated burro.

Welcome to Death Valley

As I approached what passed for a town in Death Valley appropriately named Stovepipe Wells, one establishment, I was shocked to see gas over FIFTY CENTS, but no other choice. On the other hand, I took barely three gallons.

Entering Nevada, I had accumulated enough miles on the little Dream to require the 500mile service so I found a Honda dealer. Motorcycle dealers were different in those days, informal maybe just a one car garage. The Nevada owner/mechanic not only let me watch, but taught me how to perform all the routine maintenance. I remember being more impressed with Nevada women, than California Girls. I guess it's like the difference between Bailey Quarters and Jennifer on WKRP in Cincinnati. All the guys in high school drooled over glitzy platinum blonde Jennifer, Loni Anderson. I admired Bailey, in jeans, Jan Smithers, an all-around woman, like my wife, Cindy.

Las Vegas left no memory. Between Las Vegas and Hoover Dam I saw two "cowboys" by the side of the road. The first one was dressed like an Elvis impersonator in white leather with Buffalo Bob fringes, waving a huge nickel plated .45 revolver over his head, making please stop motions. At least he did not point it at me. His partner, in working cowboy clothes waved me to keep going. Somehow, I stalled the engine and was really grateful for the electric starter. I did not stop. Buffalo Elvis looked very drunk to me.

Much of Arizona is desolate, fly-over country. Not a lot to report until Grand Canyon, but that was a must see. I'm glad I saw it then when I could ride the South Rim from overlook to overlook and look over without having to first find a parking space then walk three miles. The parking lots were already paved over with motorhomes. They didn't have to stay outside the park then. I moved on. There is lots of scenery, but most of it is just right at 50 mph. I pulled off at an overlook in the Navajo reservation. A small boy maybe 9-years-old handed me a card that said, "If you give me 25 cents to take my picture, I can buy clothes for school." I did. Somewhere on the reservation I remember a sign, "Next gas 96 miles." I was not sure I could make it and worried a lot the last lonely 20 miles. I wondered, if I ran out could a trucker take me and the bike to the next reliable petrol stand?

Navajo boy

Four Corners was a sort of tourist draw although there was nothing there then, but a plaque in the ground with a short inscription. I took a self-portrait of myself in 5 states, Utah, Colorado, New Mexico, Arizona and Hysteria. Last time I was there, 50 years later, it looked like the day after a swap meet. Half the 50 kiosks were abandoned. A woman, presumably Navajo, maybe Hopi was doing sand painting then with no tools but amazing dexterity

Me in Five States at one time, Arizona, Colorado, New Mexico, Nevada and hysteria

I had this romantic notion of riding my bike along the Denver and Rio Grande narrow gauge right of way from Durango to Silverton. Trains were not running that early in the season. I found the D&RGW roundhouse in Durango and wandered around for an hour without being disturbed. No security, I guess everything about the railroad is too heavy and too esoteric to steal. It is not as interesting without someone knowledgeable to ask about things or someone to ask me questions.

I got to wander around the roundhouse, too bad
there was no guide.

I had thought about installing a larger rear sprocket for off road, but the enclosed chain made that too much for my skill and tools. Common sense prevailed and I decided riding the Million Dollar Highway to Silverton was more doable that the narrow-gauge railroad. The roadbed for the 3-foot gauge is really narrow. There was a billboard on the way out of Durango that pointed out that the blackened hillside behind it was the result of a forest fire in 1899, be careful. The ride turned out to be more of a challenge than I expected. The Honda's little carburetor was calibrated for sea level. It was a real struggle involving constant shifting to find an RPM that would provide enough torque to keep moving. In the Rockies in those days, you saw a lot of billboard ads for superchargers to compensate for the thin air above 8000 feet. In the days when the highway was built a million dollars was real money. The 50-mile, Million Dollar, highway was built on low grade gold ore, so low grade that it was not worth the cost to haul it out and refine it. For comparison, the 2001 Century Freeway in LA cost a million dollars a foot! My thin windbreaker was proving to be inadequate and I resolved to add a sweater.

Silverton was another time warp. Even without the 1880 narrow gauge train it felt like nothing was there that wasn't there in 1880 except the tourist's cars and a huge billboard. The billboard said there is more gold, silver, copper (and many other ores) in the mountains around Silverton than has ever been mined, but again, so remote it's not worth the cost to haul it out, yet.

After Silverton the grades were not so steep and the bike made it to Monarch Crest on the Continental Divide. With one stop at Bear Creek Falls. The high altitude and low temperatures cause the mist around the falls to freeze form a bridge around the waterfall. The bridge was curved sideways. As soon as I came to a real town where people live, I bought that sweater, but he rest of the trip nothing was ever as cold as the 11,000-foot pass and I could have done without. It was comforting to have it.

Bear Creek Falls, note the natural ice bridge and
rainbow, bottom

I stopped at night in small towns. I found a clean room once for $2, I think it was Lubbock Texas. The sign said: The Price Is Right. The towns are different, but also amazingly similar. Addresses in America in 1965 were easy to find. I would stop at the first phone booth, and back then they were plentiful. The phone books were often no bigger than a high school term paper, once a single page, one side taped to the glass. Finding an address was easy in those days most towns had a grid, streets in one direction were numbered and the other way alphabetical, like downtown San Diego. Not like today where major highways, huge shopping centers and planned communities with winding streets break up the pattern. I had my military orders and my medical records with me and was able to stop in Ft. Collins Colorado and pick up my April pay!

At night I would remove the baffles from the mufflers and play bad boy for a while cruising Main Street and noticing how much this town was like the last one. I never learned how- to pick-up girls though, so it was mainly a waste of time. One girl talked to me about my behavior but nothing came of it. Things stand out that I can't place any more like a diner that had American Flyer trains running continuously around the room on a shelf near the ceiling. I think it was in Kansas.

There is a reason the middle of the US is called fly over country. The interstate highway system was in its early years and I had no trouble staying on older less hectic 2 lane highways, like US 40. I remember signs on US 40 in Kansas, "Dangerous curve ahead", "Slow down", "This means you" and "Speed limit 15". I never found the curve, but Midwestern highways often jog at right angles as much as 100 yards left or right as they follow the section boundaries necessary to fit square plots on a spherical planet. The roads started out as animal trails, with no thought about cornering speeds. It was more important to not encroach on crop land.

There were a lot of towns that consisted of a grain elevator, a CoOp, gas station, and a church. The only difference from town to town was the denomination on the church. Sometimes the CoOp was also a grocery. If the town was really big there might be a super market and a farm implement dealer. As I left one town, I could soon see the grain elevator of the next. They were spaced about a day's buggy ride apart. Somewhere in the middle country I had my first encounter with bridge deck gratings. To save weight on drawbridges the deck is steel grating instead of concrete or asphalt pavement. The way motorcycle tires wander makes the California rain grooves seem insignificant. I eventually learned to meander across the width of the lane instead of trying to ride in a straight line. Fortunately, I never had a cop watching to think I was drunk.

Motorcycle shops remained quaint. I think it was one of the I states that I stopped where the receptionist looked out of place behind the greasy parts counter/main office in a white pinafore with tiny blue flowers. The counter was decorated with two pistons; a soup bowl sized one from a diesel locomotive held a bottle cap size piston from a 50cc motorcycle.

In Indiana I had my first encounter with law enforcement. I missed a turn and had to make a U. I thought I was careful but just as I began the turn a car seemed to come out of nowhere. My front tire touched the side of the car, knocking the bike out from under me. A police officer appeared immediately enough that I could think it was a trap if that was not so absurd. After much discussion we settled the matter on the spot for $20 to the driver. I suspect he did not want it on his record either. After that the bike had a slight steering bias to the right.

My Uncle Joe lived in Greensburg Pennsylvania. Great place to stop. Uncle Joe was a regular Mark Trail or John Muir who married a trophy wife Dotty who was an all-around woman like the Bailey Quarters character. She had been married to money and had walked away from it. Great cook of course. Joe settled down and became, in his own words a bureaucrat, a county agricultural extension agent. He got paid to tell old farmers what the government thought they should do. Joe liked to brag "I got something money can't buy...poverty". I caught Dotty cleaning my bubble shield and panicked that she might be using something that would scratch the soft plastic, but it was OK. They made 3 knockout beautiful practical straight A student daughters. Plus one more that came with Dotty.

Getting closer to home changed the trip from exploration to just get there already. I found myself Singing Six Days On The Road, Dave Dudley, and not maybe paying attention until a PA State policeman pulled me over. He gave me a long lecture but when I explained why I had this long piece of paper folded down to three digits instead of a license plate he shrugged and said "If California is that screwed up, I'm not going to get involved" and just left.

I missed a turnpike exit and stopped just a little too far. I did not want to push the bike back, or drive on to the next one, so I tried to drive over the elevated gore. I made it, but swore never to try that again.

My brother was enrolled at Penn State, so I decided to visit since it was right on the way. I walked into his dorm room and asked the tall gangly kid for Mike Obenski and he said "Ken don't you recognize me?" He had grown about a foot without gaining an ounce. I don't remember what we talked about, but it's probably predictable. I also learned that a girl I was interested in was visiting too, so I arranged to visit with her outside the frat house party where she was with her cousin. She was the daughter of my Mothers best friend; my Mother had a dozen or so best friends, maybe two dozen. The bike would not start. I had no idea what to do, so out of desperation I took the spark plugs out and replaced them with another used set. The bike started right up. This became a pattern; rotate the plugs every time the bike would not start. We sat on the bike at curbside drinking cokes. This was basically my first date with Mimi, who became my first wife.

I remembered her from the day we took her family on Pop's boat and I had driven like a damn teenager, which I was, to impress her. Wrong impression, but she forgave me. In fact, she had sent a photo to Korea and said she hoped I would remember her.

When I arrived at my parent's house the first to greet me was my brother's dog. This was the most enthusiastic greeting I have ever received, from anyone ever. Duchess jumped and rolled and barked like the messiah had returned bearing gold, frankincense and meatballs. Dogs may not have the sense of time that we do, but that dog must have thought me dead and was totally amazed to see me again. She was my brother's dog, but we had played a lot.

In ten days, I had used up the 12 month or 4,000 mile warranty. I also learned that motorcycle tires do not last, and got a lot of weird advice from people who pretend to know what they are talking about with sesquipedalian expressions like "acceleration retardation" that I think they just made up. Either way, I needed tires. Some bikes use front tires faster some rear. Sometimes mail-order tires come in threes, knowing you will need two of one before the other wears out. It often means buying two even though only one is worn out, but the other is more than half gone. Some sellers warn that mixing old and new can lead to instability without explaining what that really means. I never had a problem as long as both tires had decent tread. I only ever owned one bike with tires that could be rotated. This offsets the fuel economy because in spite of their small size the tires cost as much as car tires but seldom last 20,000miles. If you can't remount them yourself you are limited to the motorcycle dealers' noncompetitive rates. Motorcycles have a short life expectancy. Not that modern ones wear out, they get crashed early. A BMW or Gold Wing can easily go 200,000 miles. Harleys seem to be always repairable so they last forever.

My professional partner of many years later, John Fiske Brown was someone who had been a mechanic, an engineer and a professor. As an expert witness we called him threefer. He could testify whether a claim is consistent with theory, good design and maintainability in the real world. He told me that the problem is that half the mechanics are incompetent and half are dishonest. Good luck. Even the best often operate under delusions. For example, how many times have you been told that a broken metal part had crystallized. Every piece of solid metal crystallized the day it was made. That is what makes it solid metal. If it was not crystalized it would not be metal. What they are calling crystallization might be metal fatigue or not, it depends on many properties. It takes some expertise in metallurgy to determine if a failure is due to fatigue, stress or an incipient defect. Most metal parts are ductile and will deform noticeably before they break. Try to break a paper clip, ductile. High strength parts less so and can break with little distortion, like glass or china. Maybe that kind of BS is why so many people don't trust mechanics.

To complete the coast to coast, SF to NYC, mission I went to visit some cousins in New York. From the Verrazano Bridge you can see the Atlantic Ocean, really the waves under the bridge are the Atlantic Ocean.

The Honda was cheaper than other bikes for a few reasons. Instead of two telescoping fork-legs, that require precision machining of high strength aluminum it had a rigid sheet steel front fork with a simple double leading link suspension like some fat tire bicycles. The wheel travel was pretty short.

Motorcycle with right-side-up telescopic forks.

To save money, early Japanese bikes were assembled with Phillip's head screws. Phillip's have the advantage that they can be installed with a high-speed power screwdriver. The driver will "cam-out" and are the screws are not easily over-tightened. Unfortunately, after a steel screw has been in an aluminum part for a few hundred heat cycles it is very hard to remove. If you don't have an impact wrench you will probably just strip the head. Further repair gets very expensive, sometimes requiring drilling it out and re-tapping the threads, if it can be repaired at all. Some owners replaced the Phillip's with hexagonal socket head, aka Allen screws.

Honda did innovate an improvement on the alternating twin configuration where the pistons rose to the top at the same time, with each cylinder firing every other time. This was called perfect primary balance with a power pulse every 360 degrees. Unfortunately, balancing the crankshaft with pistons moving in unison was not much of an improvement on the thumper and the alternating twins earned nicknames like Birmingham vibrator for the BSA motorcycle (Birmingham Small Arms). Setting the crankpins 180 degrees apart instead of together made it possible for one piston to nearly balance the other, and the crankshaft being almost inherently balanced because the counter weights are on opposite sides. This achieved almost perfect secondary balance with the flywheel absorbing the pulses of the cylinders firing at 180 degrees then 540 degrees. The overall affect was smoother. It turns out that primary balance is not so primary.

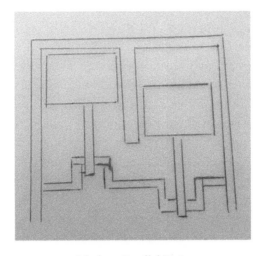

Modern Parallel Twin

Assigned to Fort Bragg I definitely felt like a fifth wheel. When you arrive at a new post in the Army, they assign you a bunk in a common room with 40 or so people you do not know, chores no one wants to do, most of which are busy work and you get no locker. Your valuables rest in your canvass duffle bag on the floor. After a few days I was assigned to an Engineering company. Yeah! Oops the Company had orders to ship to Vietnam. Fortunately, because I had just returned from Korea, which the Army classified as a short tour (hardship) area, I could elect not to go to another short tour area for at least a year. I did not volunteer. I spent a few months helping them pack. Mostly this consisted of sitting in a warehouse telling stories if we had one. Occasionally patching something with what we called "Army green tape" the original duck-tape. Tape made from cotton duck cloth.

For the next year the Dream was my primary mode of transportation between Hatboro, Pennsylvania in the Philadelphia suburbs and Fort Bragg, North Carolina, 485 miles. That's a long day on a saddle. I made that trip several times a year in a wide range of weather conditions. Once it was so cold. I gave up at the first rest area and slept on a picnic table with my feet in my laundry bag until morning.

Romance at one end and duty at the other made the trip necessary, at least in my mind.

Having wheels at both ends of the trip made a lot of exploration possible. Although the military location made social events limited for me. North Carolina is a beautiful place to explore with two-lane country roads attractive for motorcycles. I explored many as well as the quaint small-town nodes.

The long commute encouraged me to push the bike's limits and I found myself prone on the gas tank with my ankles crossed behind me to minimize drag. Although the bikes top end was maybe 75, I achieved an indicated 105 once drafting a big Ford diesel highway tractor downhill. It's possible the vibration pushed the speedometer needle up.

At the northern end of the commute, I visited family and my future wife Mimi. One time in spite of her parent's disapproval we took an all-day ride south from Philly to the Eastern Shore of the Chesapeake Bay and back. One of those rare days that lives up to the "You meet the nicest people" idea. Japanese bikes all came with a crude set of cheesy tools that you can do basic maintenance with. They still do, but the set has fewer tools now. There is usually a compartment for them. In the case of the Dream it was a shelf above the battery with a sheet metal cover secured by one screw that had a plastic knob instead of a hex head. At the beginning of the day trip the cover fell off and the tools got lost, that of course was frustrating and I wanted to blame my passenger as if she could have at least noticed it fall off, but in reality, it was behind and below her leg and I managed to let it pass.

The Eastern Shore likes to call itself the land of pleasant living, and it seemed idyllic then. A land of small towns, chicken farms and fishing. We found a beach to relax on and before heading home, watch the ships passing by on the Delaware Bay, a surprising large number of them. There is definitely an attraction to riding together cuddled on a bike, cuddled instead of side by side in a car. I applied the brakes a little harder than necessary to enhance the contact. The day trip was only marred by an incident on the Baltimore Avenue trolley tracks when we were almost home. I crossed the tracks at too shallow an angle and one wheel got momentarily caught in the flange-way causing the bike wobble violently. Her feet flew off the pegs, flailed wildly and one calf impacted on the foot-peg. It was good I had insisted she get boots.

Like most big cities Philadelphia had parking problems. There was an unwritten policy with the Philly Police. If a motorcycle was parked on the sidewalk, but left 5 feet for pedestrians to pass there would be no parking ticket. Most houses had a stoop that projected far enough to make compliance easy. Another unwritten law in Philly was, if a motorcycle gets a traffic ticket, he gets it in the mail. I never got one.

I got an on-base speeding ticket though. Military justice is of course an oxymoron. In this case it was adjudicated in the First Sergeant's office. First offense, I got off with a lecture. Maybe the First-Shirt thought that would endear me to the company and I would volunteer to go with them to 'Nam.

Military justice: One day about six of us were relaxing in the shade of the barracks when an officer started to walk by. In the Corps of Engineers, we did not salute Warrant Officers, but he was Major. The insignia are hard to tell apart at a distance. He picked on one Spec-5, not me, to lecture but didn't pursue it. Actually, I was senior but did not argue. The Corps of Engineers was the least Army part of the army. Again, no real discipline resulted.

One day I noticed that the Honda's chain adjustment had reached its limit, I had a chain breaker (disassembly) tool, so I took out two links.

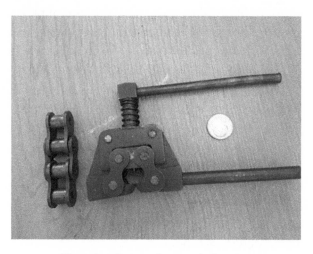

Chain breaker used to pry links apart

It is not practical to take out one, because they alternate in configuration, inner-outer. Like a bicycle chain, but bigger. I put it back together, not knowing in my naiveté that running the lengthened links was ruining the sprockets.

I discovered a crack in the rear fender, and tried to get it fixed in Fayetteville but no welder in the area would mess with Japanese steel. The next trip home my Dad and I fixed the crack by riveting a piece of sheet metal across it. While we were at it, we cobbled up a windshield and front fairing that went all the way down to the front axle. I know today that that could have been very unstable, but I got away with it. It made it look like a 1930 diesel locomotive, but it worked.

I had a flat tire on the rear, while I had a large passenger; I think it was Clem my buddy from Korea, fresh from Vietnam. I can't recall how he too got to Fort Bragg, but I don't think he was in the same outfit. Rear flats are scary because the rear wanders. If you keep the front pointed where you want to go and you don't have

52

to brake hard you can safely stop. The tube was destroyed so I had to replace it. The offending object was still in the tire, a safety pin, an average size safety pin. Each time the tire went around it made a new hole in the tube. I don't know about front flats because I have still not had one! When I asked more experienced riders what to do if I had a front flat the only answer I ever got was: you will know when it happens. My experience is that most flats are on the rear. The explanatory theory is that nails are lying flat. The front tire kicks them up and sometimes they land on the head just in time to be run over by the rear. My off-road Guru, Harry, subscribes to the same theory relative to 4x4 flats. I have noticed that rock cuts in the sidewall happen more to front tires. I think that because the front makes a bigger circle it's more likely to find a sharp rock. The front might get cut knocking the rock aside.

One can quickly make friends with other riders. I hooked up with one in in North Carolina, and we rode together for a while. I decide that was not a good plan when he tried to pass me as I made a left turn, we missed by about three inches. Some riders are all about speed, sometimes I am and other times I just explore.

The Army transferred me to the 1st and 42nd Artillery. Artillery needs surveyors. Once the surveyors figure out the exact location of each gun, the guns can be amazingly accurate. The first round they fire will probably miss, but the Forward Observer, (FO) an officer positioned where he can see the target, will estimate the error and the gunner will adjust. The second round will be much closer and the FO and the gunner now know what a grad of adjustment at the gun is worth at the target. A grad is one yard difference at a thousand yards range. I observed a howitzer battery in Korea hit an outhouse dead center from five miles away. This is where the surveyors become really important. They make it possible for each gunner to know his exact position relative to the others and everything else. The next instruction is "fire for effect" then every single gun can hit the same spot, or any other designated target in the area with a single round. That is pre-electronics; it's all done with iron and glass. A radio helps.

It was during a Christmas trip home without the bike that many states including Pennsylvania decided to require a special motorcycle driver's license endorsement. I needed to take the test right away, but it was winter and I was one place and my bike another. I had a friend Dave with a 350 Yamaha. I thought that would do, since the test never gets out of first gear. One of the relatively absurd requirements was to make a U-turn in a narrow stall. That is narrow relative to a car. Very easy, except there were patches of ice in the stall and I had to dodge them. Dave watched me from the lobby and thought I rode like a drunk.

I filed a 1049 request for transfer monthly. The form number is sardonically similar to the IRS 1040. I was hoping to get back in the Corps of Engineers where they do useful things and don't march. One trip between Ft. Bragg and Philly I stopped at Ft. Belvoir, it was an open post in those pre-9/11 days, no fences. Driving through it on US 1 was like driving through a park. Dropped in on the 30th Engineering Battalion (topo base) talked to the Assistant First Sergeant, we just called Van, the kind of NCO you could talk to like your uncle. I told him that there were 12 Topographic Surveyors stuck in an artillery group at Ft. Bragg. That could have gotten me in major trouble for insubordination, or mutiny, but instead it got me and several others transferred where we belonged. The 30th was the least army unit in the Army. My 3 months in the 1st and 42nd entitles me to wear the Croix De Guerre, (Often mispronounced something like foe-re-jair) France's highest honor, on my uniform. It is a unit citation, so anyone ever assigned to that battalion gets to wear it. It's like being the pizza delivery guy to a movie location; your name is on the credits forever even after it wins an Oscar. Of course, considering the reputation of the French military getting their top award is like being the smartest bear in the zoo. It tells you something when their most honored military unit is the Foreign Legion: composed of not Frenchmen and their most famous leader a teenage girl.

I was not at Belvoir long before there was an opportunity and I volunteered for a TDY (Temporary Duty) field assignment and nominated my new best friend Jack to fill the last open spot. I had been at Belvoir before for my own advanced individual training. As a Topographic Surveyor.

Jack and I were assigned to the same surveying platoon even though we had entirely different backgrounds. Since he was drafted for only two years the Army did not send him to advanced individual training.

Back to the 30th. Six of us would go to San Diego as virtual civilians to assist Cubic Corporation in developing a new technology. We were paid per diem for expenses and lived in motels. I lovingly stored my Honda at my uncle's house. Changed the oil, shot oil through the plug holes, oiled the chain. Greased things and everything else the manual said. We were gone a month. I actually got to do more Topographic Surveying in that month than my year and a half as a Topographic Surveyor in the 161 in Korea. We set up on a hilltop outside Yuma and tracked an airplane with our theodolite while synchronized cameras photographed the internal protractors. We did that two nights. We were measuring the total straight line distance from San Diego to Yuma.

Directly measuring the distance from San Diego to Yuma

Mostly we watched TV, there was only one channel in Yuma. We also played Monopoly. Yuma then was a typical southwestern town ten miles long and one street wide. We walked the strip looking for something to do and found a bar with no one in it, not even a bartender. The most active night life we found was at the airport bar. Yuma International Airport! Three flights a week to Mexico.

One night we decided to go check out San Luis Mexico. Typical border town that caters to Gringo sin. On the way back the Border Patrol asked me to open the trunk. Uh Oh in the. Trunk were three clearly labeled U S Army radios. By taking them across the border we were in violation of some treaty between the US and Mexico, not to mention the problem we would have with the Army if the radios got lost. I started to explain the presence of U S Army electronics in a civilian rent-a-car but he interrupted me with "I don't want to get involved" and sent us across.

During that month we decided to sneak out so Jack could visit his wife Becky in San Angelo, Texas. I was the only one authorized to drive the rental car so I drove 1200 miles almost non-stop, gas and take-out food. The Pleiades meteor shower was that night. Dick in the back seat counted over 600 shooting stars. One was so close we could hear it! It lit up the car like a lightning storm. We stopped and tried to find the meteorite, but when it hit it must not have been as close as it appeared. Close enough that we could see glowing fragments breaking off the main body. It looked as big as a car. The mass looked partly black and partly red hot. Pieces shooting off looked hotter, yellow to white. I think I could smell it.

We got to sleep at about 6 AM. At 8AM we got a call to be back in San Diego ASAP so I drove another 1400 miles almost non-stop. Half way back I threw a tire tread. The original equipment tires were not really good for sustained 90 mph. I felt obligated to replace the tire ASAP so we would not fail to return. The Army is fussy about showing up. The tire cost $21 at a gas station. The rental agency complained that I spent so much when they get tires for $7. Well maybe if they spent a little more their tires would not fall apart.

Back at Ft. Belvoir; On my way back from a date I got a motorcycle speeding ticket in Washington D.C. on a freeway with a 35mph speed limit! The officer said I was going twice the limit and he might have noticed I had had a few beers also. He got my address right but wrote up my California License plate as Maryland, they were the same color that year. Remember when we got a new one every year? I paid it anyway because getting military leave to go to traffic court can work out badly.

It was necessary in those days to always carry cash because many gas stations would not allow a motorcyclist to use a credit card. They claimed the processing cost exceeded the profit on a dollars-worth.

The next TDY assignment was unusual and would last a year. The Army sent us to do a topographic survey of a large piece of real estate you may have heard of, it's called Arizona. The Army was going to pay my mileage to drive to Arizona, so I decided it was time to buy a car. I chose Volkswagen because it was the cheapest new car. The car needed certain service to preserve the warranty. Probably my Dad or Brother drove me home when I took the car in but was not available to drive me back to get it. I rode the bike to the dealer, but I had to move the bike and the VW home from the dealer. Because it had the double leading link front end, I could take the wheel off, set the links on the VW bumper, tie it down and tow it like a trailer. That worked perfectly.

Leading Link front suspension (BMW, Honda had much
shorter links)

Unfortunately, the next time I rode the bike and had to stop something was wrong. I had missed one of the connections and when I applied the brakes, instead of the brakes stopping the wheel, the brake foundation rotated on the axle. This broke the brake cable anchor and that released the brakes. I crashed into a car, but at such a low speed there was no subsequent damage. The way the anchor broke I could still reconnect it and it worked fine once I also connected the torque link I had overlooked. The Dream front brakes were pretty primitive type called leading, trailing where a single cam operated both shoes against a single fixed anchor. Not uncommon for the parking brake on a car. That was the only problem I ever had with them, but I only kept the bike 12,000 miles. I took my bike home to Hatboro, and parked it with no prep. Winter was coming.

I drove West by way of Gary Indiana near Chicago so my friend Tom who had also been in the First and Forty-second, could visit home. It snowed the night we got there. We were caught in the blizzard-of-the-century. The Army does not accept excuses. We had to leave on time. The roads were slippery, but thankfully the rear engine VW handled it with aplomb. On the freeway, I 55 there were big rigs on their sides everywhere. I wore two pair of sunglasses to improve the contrast so I could find the road. Somewhere in southern Illinois the V Dub stopped running. I had no idea what was wrong, but I looked at the ignition points and they seemed to be stuck closed. I pried them open and the car started. Much later I learned that the point arm had cracked. It was a miracle that it would run. Somewhere outside St Louis we decided to quit for the night and look for a place to stay after driving 400 miles in a blizzard on the freeway, I got stuck in a ditch on a country road. It looked like we were stuck for the night when a local man the size of a grizzly bear picked up the heavy end of the VW, put it back on the road and disappeared.

The Army got us to Globe AZ in a hurry then had us wait a couple of months while someone somewhere figured out exactly what we were supposed to do. That's the Army way, hurry up and wait. We were issued every Army owned commercial pickup truck and M38A1 Jeep in the western states that was on its last legs. M38A1 was the first one with a rounded hood, but otherwise looked pretty much every jeep from 1941 to 1960. Up until then the only Jeeps I had experience with were the notorious M151. The Ford M151 was lower than the older jeeps and handled like a sports car, unfortunately most people can't really drive sportscars properly (sportscars oversteer) so the M151 would get sideways and then a rear wheel would tuck under and flip the jeep, like a Corvair®. M38s handled like a dump truck (they understeer). They would go into a wild spin when out of control and the spin stabilized them like a Frisbee so they stayed right side up as they went off the road backwards. Army jeeps like motorcycles have no seat belts. This may seem crazy, but the logic is since you are on the outside its better to be tossed off and left behind than be attached to a vehicle that can flip over on top of you, more than once.

Two of our teams did just that. In one case the passenger walked away and ran miles to get help. The driver was pinned to the seat by the steering wheel on the first roll. Then the jeep rolled over and over on top of him. He was hospitalized for six months. I almost did the same thing, but knocked the jeep out of gear as I bailed out and it just fell back on its wheels. Bailed from the high side. My passenger bailed from the low side and was fortunate the jeep did not flip onto him.

It is counter instinctive to recover control in a vehicle like an M151 that oversteers. When it feels like it is going off the road the trick is to steer less and give it more power, but never brake. In some ways this is like learning to ride a bike. Turning the intuitive way makes it worse.

When I was a new driver in a '50 Studebaker with badly worn tires I was rounding a sharp curve on a slick road and felt the oversteer. Something told me gas it. I did and the car stabilized. Fortunately, the little six-cylinder did not make enough power to spin the wheels or I would have gone off the road backwards into a deep gorge with a railroad track.

The Army provided a collection of state-of-the-art surveying equipment, T3 theodolites, Microchains® and Telurometers® that can measure any distance 10 yards to ten miles with an accuracy of one centimeter. We got almost none of the essentials like canteens and backpacks. Our job was called third order picture point recovery. We would be sent eight by ten stereo contact prints of aerial photographs. Each one had a tiny pinhole made from the back designating a feature, picture point, we were to find and then locate exactly according to the US Geological Survey grid. These photos were taken from 24,000 feet and it was possible on the photos to find a barbed wire fence using the stereoscope - a two-lens magnifier that worked like the stereopticon your grandmother had. A picture-point was something the compilers at Army Map Service though would be visible from space, usually an intersection of two roads or gullies. Sometimes it was just a one particular rock in a field of rocks. Sometimes you see a picture- point alongside a highway, a painted plus sign.

Once we found a picture-point we had to determine which mountain top had a line-of- sight view of it. Then determine what other mountain top could be seen from that one. Haul our equipment to all three locations at the same time and make the necessary measurements. Why was this done? It made it possible to calibrate satellite cameras so the military and now Google Earth could produce high quality photo and topographic maps of any place on Earth. Satellite mapping was in its infancy. The Soviet Embassy used to buy maps of the USSR from Army Map Service in Arlington Virginia because KGB paranoiac editing made the official Soviet maps useless. That's what the Army told us and I have independent confirmation.

Climbing a mountain every day made me fantasize about a motorcycle that could do it. These were untamed mountains, no improved trails, just deer trails, but plenty of rattlesnakes. As Jack and I were walking down from one of the peaks I heard a rattlesnake buzz: between my feet! The traditional wisdom is that when one encounters a rattlesnake, to freeze, but I was 20 yards away before I even knew why. After our heartbeats got close to normal, we went back and killed the poor defenseless reptile. Not the first or last that we dispatched. I bought a .22 revolver and loaded it with #12 dust shot. Years later I was watching a movie that that exploited that sound. It made me jump out of my seat several times.

We had a sergeant nicknamed Rat. He had to have a double bourbon every 20 minutes to get through the day. First thing in the morning and all day. If his drinking was interrupted, say driving from Mammoth to Globe, he needed a double-double after 40 minutes. Lots of strange people in the Army.

Reminds me of more strange people in the Army. Sgt. Bean, guess what he drank?

Joined the Army to avoid prosecution after he broke a bridge with an overloaded truck.

Captain Brown, now there is an all-American Name for a CO, guys would follow wherever. A good CO feels like second father. He was a helicopter pilot and known for his extreme maneuvers. He wanted to know if a helicopter could fly upside down, but had enough sense to not try. Some thought he had.

Three Lieutenants, Shedrick, Loup, and Dalson. We all agreed that if the balloon went up, i.e., the excrement hit the ventilator we would all follow Loup no matter whose platoon we were supposed to be in so we would have a chance of survival.

Dennis was the kind you expected to get into trouble or make trouble and he did, from falling into a honey ditch (open sewer) to getting bitten by a probably rabid chipmunk, complained that the business girls would not have sex face to face on their side.

You meet a lot of assholes in the Army, Cummings our third CO was the most extreme. Son of a Colonel he tried to be important but instead made things worse. During a proficiency test of nuclear weapons, he got a sudden urge to open a window and almost knocked the dummy detonator out of my hand. I wish to this day that I had dropped or fumbled it. He had us spend hours filling in the blank spaces on stenciled truck letters, for which he then got gigged, along with a lot of other motor-pool deficiencies, like painting the tool handles, painting mufflers or having oil overfilled. That can cause the engine to begin to leak. We had no paint brushes, and paint only in 5gallon cans. We improvised with tin cans and cigarette filter brushes.

My last month in the Army was spent at Belvoir with little to do. When you are short, that is close to separation they cut you a little slack. I had to visit a lot of offices staffed by civilians. I could not help but notice there was a peculiarity in office staff hiring. It seemed everywoman I saw, old or young, fat or thin was wearing the same style very pointy bra.

With time on my hands, I could pass it in what they call the day room. Usually, part of the facility was divided into three television rooms, for the three networks. If there was a football game on, all three TVs would be on the same game. I think this was because the fans would congregate by team plus some other commonality and commandeer a room.

The price of gas went up a lot that year $1.299 a gallon. I finally had to put two dollars- worth in a motorcycle tank. I soon sold the bike. It had about 12,000 miles on it and a noise in the engine I was told was a broken piston ring. The buyer did not mind. The last thing I did with it was one lap around the neighborhood.

I hit gravel on a sharp turn, I should have known better, and went down hard. When the potential buyer arrived, I was cleaning small rocks and asphalt emulsion out of my abrasions with a gasoline-soaked rag. He never even noticed or asked, just paid the asking price and left.

A FAMILY BMW

WE had a BMW before BMW was cool. Before most American's ever heard of BMW. Back before the Whizzer days my Dad bought a BMW Isetta®. In those days BMW cars were rare mostly tiny and were serviced by the BMW motorcycle dealers. They bought the Isetta 2- seater design from an Italian Company Iso SpA and replaced the original 1 cylinder 2 stroke motor with their more reliable four stroke motorcycle engine. This was the 3-wheel car you might remember that the whole front opened up. Actually, if you looked closely there were two rear wheels, very close together. BMW also designed a 4-seater 4-wheel version with a 500cc 2-cylinder opposed four-stroke engine. More about that later. It was the easiest car ever to get in or out of. Open the door, stand up walk away, crashworthiness somewhere between a motorcycle with a fairing and VW Microbus. We saw one at an exotic car dealership between the Rolls', Mercedes' and Maserati's. The little BMW Isetta was the only car on the showroom floor without an oil stain under it, not even a drip pan or newspaper. The 4-seater four-wheel version, a differential and handled like a sports car. It was fun to drive. In fact, they later rebodied the chassis into a 700cc sports car. I coveted one.

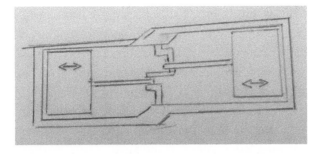

Horizontally opposed "boxer" engine, 2 to 6 cylinders

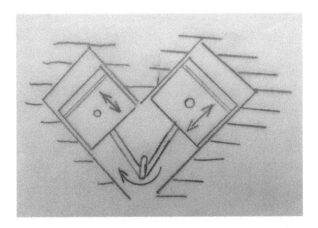

Typical 90degreeV engine, 2 to 16 cylinders

The Isetta introduced us to BMW engines and motorcycles. The engine is an opposed twin, sometimes called a boxer, with one cylinder on each side. Half a VW or original Porsche engine. Each cylinder is a mirror image of the other. The crankpins are 180 degrees apart so the pistons go out and in at the same time in perfect secondary balance. The firing intervals are 360 degrees apart, left, right, left, right, so the primary balance is also perfect. The short crankshaft itself is almost perfectly balanced too. It hardly needs counterweights. The engine is almost as smooth as a V8. A Harley owner once asked me "How can you tell it's running?

"I started it."

The BMW motorcycle had a shaft drive like a car. The WWII BMW sidecar motorcycle had power to both rear wheels. It was probably less of a beast to ride than other 1WD rigs. It has been copied by Russian, Japanese, Chinese and other German builders that I know of. (*Dnieper, Ural, Marusho, Great Wall* and *Zundapp*), Even Harley built an opposed twin, but with the cylinders fore and aft, the crankshaft crosswise and chain drive. The rear cylinder behind the crankcase was not in the airflow and overheated.

BMW was originally an aircraft engine builder. WWI reparations almost put them out of business, they were reduced to making wheelbarrows. In 1923 they made their first motorcycle, the R32. A boxer twin with a driveshaft instead of a chain. It was revolutionary. After WWII they lost their car factory to the Soviet sector. They concentrated on motorcycles. BMW came to be called the Rolls Royce of motorcycles. By 1970 Rolls Royce had lost its aura, but not BMW.

When I returned from Korea, my brother had found a 1960 BMW R60, 600cc motorcycle that he wanted to buy. He asked me to test ride it for him and I found it OK so that became the second Beemer in the family. He had his own adventure with it. The one that comes to mind was when the State Police were stopping scores of motorcycles for noise violations. He waited for his turn. The officer said "OK start it up"

Mike said "It's still running." Case over. BMW showed that motorcycles could be clean, quiet and reliable when other motorcycles were noisy, shaky, unreliable and dripped oil everywhere. Another advantage to the boxer twin was that the cylinders were horizontal which made the cooling fins vertical. They could idle much longer without overheating because convection cooling works better that way. Most vertical twins were truly vertical. That meant the cooling fins were horizontal and hardly worked at all if the bike was stationary. Honda partly overcame the problem by tilting the "vertical" twin slightly forward.

The 1960 R60, I bought from my brother. April in
State College, PA.

I had the opportunity to discuss airflow and engine cooling
with an aeronautics engineer. I was concerned about the bikes crash
bars interfering with cooling. He told me that the crash bars caused
the air to behave as the wake of two cylinders, increasing turbulence
for improved cooling. That also explained why the rear cylinder
on a V-twin Harley did not overheat, it operated in the turbulent
wake of the front cylinder. I once asked about cooling the middle
cylinder of three-cylinder bikes. It turns out the middle cylinder,
in the turbulent wake of the front wheel runs a little cooler than its
sisters. The opposite of what you would suspect.

One day at home a year later I asked Mike if I could take a ride
on the R60. He warned me that the front brake was disconnected
because it was badly worn. That was the day I learned how useless
the rear brake is. A car in front of me stopped and I was barely able
to avoid crashing my brother's bike. He got a lecture about brakes
and safety. The front brake on that was a sophisticated for-its-time
double leading shoe. Leading shoes have the cam or cylinder on
the end that moves forward relative to the rotating drum. The
friction helps push the shoe against the fixed anchor multiplying
the available force. Self-energizing is the term of art. Having
both shoes leading greatly increases the available braking effect
compared to leading, trailing where the trailing shoe contributes

half as much. It costs a little more for the secondary linkage to operate two cams instead of one. The Bendix® brakes on pre disc brake cars have an even more sophisticated single anchor double leading shoe. The primary shoe is anchored to the secondary shoe rather than a fixed pivot. The primary energizes the secondary and this made it possible to stop a ton-and-a-half (15000 pound) truck without powerbrakes.

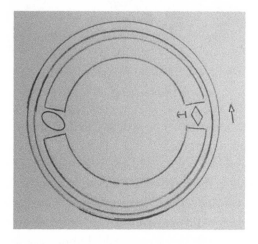

Leading Trailing Shoe Brakes, one cam, one anchor

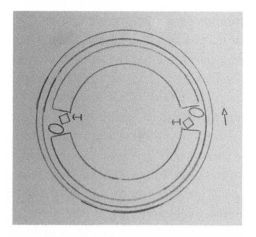

Double Double Leading Shoe brakes, 2 cams 2 anchors

The civilian truck ton designations seem to have little to do with any definition of a ton. (There are many) Ton in that contest seems to be approximately 10,000 pounds Gross Vehicle Weight Rating GVWR. A three-quarter-ton like an F250 has a GVWR of 8,550 pounds. Army trucks are rated differently and can't be compared. The classic Army deuce-and-a-half is a 2 ½ ton 6x6 truck rated for that load off-road and five tons on-road. When they say off-road, they mean no road, not just end of pavement.

That reminds me of another Army story. One of my responsibilities was to start a deuce- and-a-half every morning drive it 10 feet, back up and park it again. The truck had 5000 miles on the odometer, but it was worn out. Don't start your motor unless you are going to use it, 80% 0f the wear occurs on cold starts.

Someone had replaced the BMW mufflers with aftermarket ones called Havamuffler® because one of the original ones was damaged. One of the Havamufflers rusted out so we put the other stock muffler back on. The mismatched mufflers worked well. There was a barely detectable asymmetry to the sound, but nothing like a Harley.

Mike decided to buy a car, and I bought his R60. I had a car too, the VW, but rode the R60 most of the time. State College had motorcycle parking on College Avenue, the main street one block from the engineering buildings. They did it the right way. Two parallel parking stalls end to end will fit a dozen motorcycles. Most places do motorcycle parking by simply designating two adjacent stalls as motorcycle parking. That way two parking spaced might hold 5 bikes. The main parking lot that we called the Tundra was on the other side of the campus a mile away. Parking lot 80, the Tundra was on a plateau. If you stood on your toes, you could see the North Pole. With nothing in the way to block the wind but a few strands of barbed wire. The wind would blow you to class, but you needed help getting back. Fortunately, the sidewalks on campus were steam heated. One of the motorcycle magazines listed any road in Pennsylvania as the worst place to ride. I did not find it so and explored many a back road. How can you resist

69

names like Puddintown Road? A friend once lived there. I was not trying to see how fast, just exploring, unpaved roads and roads not yet open to the public. I even took the 550-pound R60 off road, and somehow avoided getting hopelessly stuck. One gravel road had a turn so sharp it was actually 179 degrees left. The path to follow was a right hand 179-degree loop that crossed back on itself to going back the way you came. I did some crazy things too, like passing a slow-moving tractor trailer on a sharp curve. As the long straight trailer went to the right it created a pocket between the trailer and the other side of the road. Somehow, I used that to pass a crawling truck that was too long to pass at once into two short passes.

There are a lot of Amish People in Pennsylvania. I have always found them amiable even though they mostly stay apart from us "English." The movie Witness does a pretty accurate portrayal of Amish people. Sometimes riding on very rural roads I would pass them and the young men would pretend to run alongside, one man fell down as if exhausted, rolled on the asphalt and laughed. The women would also laugh, but discreetly. On our rides we found an amazingly busy Amish store that was a bakery and saddlery. They had fantastic bread, organic before organic was cool. Amish farmers shun chemicals. Great hand-made leather goods but out of my student price range.

I have almost always worn a helmet after the Whizzer days; frankly it's more comfortable to me than the wind trying to tear my scalp off. The states started passing helmet laws and suddenly we had to worry about helmet thieves. Some bikes had helmet locks, but that only secured the D-ring (buckle) to the bike. A thief could cut the chin strap and get a free but not perfectly legal helmet. Thieves don't really concern themselves much with 'legal'. I fabricated a chin strap guard from steel tubing to make the thief work harder.

We were riding on a farm road near State College when the bike suddenly dropped out from under us. It dropped us on the paving and kept moving. There was no warning. I was upright one milli-second and lying on the road the next, watching the bike chug-chug away using the right cylinder head crash bar as a sled runner. It just kept going and going until the drag overcame the lugging engine and it stopped. When I tried to stand up I found the asphalt so slippery that it was impossible, I had to crawl on all four to the gravel shoulder first. Fortunately, the bike came to a stop where it ran out of oiled pavement. It still took two of us to right it again because the road was still slippery, just not perfectly so. Some old farm machinery leaks a lot of oil and there is sometimes not enough rain and traffic agitation to eliminate it. Thanks to the after-market crash bar the engine valve cover was protected and the only damage was cosmetic.

Some things you learn unexpectedly. The bike was running rough and I suspected water in the gas. I disconnected the fuel line from one carburetor, put a disposable cup under the hose, opened a valve and gasoline splashed on my foot. Hmm I didn't notice that the cup had a hole in it. Got another cup, inspected this one carefully. Repeated the test and got the same result. Gasoline dissolves Styrofoam, instantly. It's like the Styrofoam anticipates the gasoline and makes an opening to avoid contact. Water however does not, so what came out of the hose was just gas.

I never learned how to do the maintenance properly (to install the condenser you had to solder, and I did not have a timing light or dwell meter) The engine always started on the first kick. BMW owners had been known to make and win $50 bets that the bike would start on one kick. Some other bikes needed you to "kick th' bjesus out of them." Most motorcycle crankshafts run crosswise. The kick starter shaft is parallel to the crankshaft so the kick starter pedal, is parallel to the crankshaft, perpendicular to the bike much like a bicycle pedal, and therefore made to be pushed down from the saddle, you almost have to get on first. BMW crankshaft in fact all its shafts ran fore and aft like a pickup truck's. So the kick starter pedal was parallel to the frame and made to be kicked from standing alongside. Either way works OK, and either could be started the other way but awkwardly. That bike was so easy to start in spite of the large, 72mm, pistons that I could do it with one hand.

I needed an 8mm wrench. I went to the name brand tool store and the wrench was about $8, I thought that was too much and the indignant owner behind the counter told me "You can go to Joe The Motorist and buy a whole set for $8, but they will break the second time you use them." I could not see how they would break exactly the second time, but I only needed once so I took a chance. I still have them, used them a lot and they didn't break. They are heavier and not as polished as the BMW tools or Snap On.

I did a lot of exploring on that bike. I remember being at the famous Horseshoe curve as a mile-long freight train descended with red hot brakes screaming and throwing off sparks. The Horseshoe curve of the new Pennsylvania Railroad in 1853 reduced travel time between the mid- western river transportation network and the Eastern cities from weeks to days. I got into a small town in coal country and for the first time was actually surrounded by girls asking for rides, probably not much else to do there. They looked a little young to me so I said "Sure, just get a note from your Mom" and they disappeared. When in doubt, document.

It wasn't long before I decided I wanted a windshield. Mike bought the bike with a handlebar mounted fairing that he never installed. I mounted the fairing, then went to buy some Plexiglas for a windshield. The store recommended polycarbonate half as thick because it's twice as strong therefore less expensive. If I had known then what I knew two years later. I would not have bought it. Twice as thick can be 8 times as strong. It did not work. Twice as strong, material but too thin was more flexible, the wind bent it right over, even after I reinforced it. My neighbor suggested that I was making it too high so we cut it down to just below my eyes and that sort of worked but ultimately I paid for the ¼ inch Plexiglas. That worked very well, but I kept imagining replacing the plexi with glass, maybe a VW rear window, so I could have a wiper, never did. I tend to fantasize about more improvements than I actually accomplish. I overthink and under accomplish.

In those days many motorcycle front and rear tires were the

same or about the same size and you could carry a spare front inner tube that would stretch enough to fit the rear. Tube type tires can be demounted and remounted with 6-inch tire irons that some tool kits included. BMW even made the front and rear wheels interchangeable, so theoretically you could rotate the tires and have a pair wear out at the same time. Ideal front and rear tires are not the same design and most bikes have a wider size on the rear. Sometimes the difference is extreme, 2.50x23 front and 5.00x16 rear.

We rode into New York City, the Bronx no less, to visit Mimi's Brother. The trip was unadventurous except when we arrived and I took off my motorcycle gear the exposed my face was as obviously black as a coal miner. I parked it on the sidewalk like we did in Philly and nobody complained.

The bike came with a set of aluminum bags. When they are lockable and easy to take off and put back on, they are often called panniers because it sounds more sophisticated than saddle bags which on motorcycles are usually fixed. I think pannier is French for bread basket. Horse saddle bags are usually just thrown over the horse.

There was a place called Hall's Salvage outlet (We spelled it Hauls too) that sold an odd collection of merchandise that I think came from overturned trucks, or foreclosure sales. It was between State College and Bellefonte, the county seat, about 20 miles from my trailer. Sometimes one could find an incredible bargain. One time we found a lot of good buys, stocked up, then went outside and realized we were on the bike. With a lot of ingenuity, we managed to attach everything.

I felt the need for more capacity. Also, I once almost rode the bike out from under Mimi and put her on the luggage rack, a sissy bar would be smart too. Dad had some aluminum sheet and we fabricated a trunk big enough to hold a case of beer, 24 16-ounce returnable bottles, the heavy ones, with room to spare for a sack of groceries. It worked well, but I was frequently imagining something bigger. It was probably just as well I never made it because I now know that it could have been unstable. Could have been, but that bike was a stable as a church pew, unless the road was oiled.

BMWs have a single disc dry clutch, just like cars and light trucks. If the rear seal leaks, oil can get on the clutch disc and let it slip. Generally, if a clutch slips you have to replace it. This one was unique in that it was possible to fill the clutch housing with a solvent, the preferred solvent, carbon tetrachloride, was still being used for fire extinguishers and dry-cleaning fluid. I stuffed a rag in the drain hole, poured the carbon-tet through the timing mark hole in the housing, worked the clutch a bit, with the engine running and drained the CT out. It was filthy and I think I just poured it on some weeds; we did not know better in those days. The clutch worked better; except I accidently did my first wheelie shifting from first to second. I have never really been confident (foolish) enough to accomplish that trick. Anyhow there was no further trouble with the clutch.

I read that a black painted engine would be more efficient and gain half a horsepower. I cleaned the cylinders and heads then spray painted the engine black. I could not feel any extra power, but it changes the sound! I changed it back.

BMW R60 had some unusual features, the tool compartment was built into the side of the gas tank beautifully, but in a way that must have been very trying for the production department. It even had a good lock that used the same key as the fork lock. The ignition and lights used a bulky knob and pin that looked like an RCA jack. It fit every BMW, and maybe every Model T. The bike had a hinged rear fender so you could take off the rear tire with the bike upright on the service stand instead of laying it down. Very useful on a bike designed to have a sidecar. My fender unfortunately was rusted in place so I laid the bike over if I needed to remove a wheel.

One day at home the bike started misfiring it was easy to tell from the kick-starter that one cylinder had no compression. I rode it to an independent mechanic Stan M who had a very good reputation. He figured out what I needed to do and said he was too busy, but it was an easy job. Take off two nuts, loosen two hose clamps and the exhaust pipes come right off.

Carburetor is held by hose clamps, just let it dangle on the fuel hose and throttle cable. Four bolts at the base and the entire cylinder and head come off as an assembly. Drive the piston pin out with a hammer using a socket wrench for a spacer, simple. To reinstall the piston pin, warm the piston in hot water. He sold me a new piston. It went smoothly. Those engines were easy to work on, at least the top end.

The piston had a hole in it like it had melted. The new piston actually went in more easily than expected. When I started it though, it clattered like threshing machine. I rode it to the nearest motorcycle mechanic, the local Triumph dealer to get an opinion and they told me it sounded like the new piston was too small. I took it apart and took both pistons to Stan. He noticed that my old piston was second oversize, that is about two millimeters bigger. Something none of us expected with only 60,000 on the odometer, but it could have been the second, or third, time around. BMWs can do that. The oversize piston had only increased the displacement about 4%. Not much of a performance improvement. He had a second oversize piston on hand, amazing, and took back the slightly used one. Everything went back together OK. The proper size piston took some work to get in, you have to compress the piston rings which are made to fit tightly, but it fit. There is a slight taper on the bottom of the cylinder so the rings slide in easier than from the top where there tends to be a ridge. The engine worked well.

Stan's shop was his second gig. His day job was maintaining big trucks for Philadelphia Electric. PE bought the cheapest Ford stripper sedans (not even a back seat) that they could, kept them 50,000 miles with no maintenance at all, never opened the hood then discarded them. Maintaining the expendable cheap cars was not worth it to corporate. Stan also raced BMW motorcycles, as I recall his race bike was based on a very old one that he preferred because of the cylinder head design.

Mimi and I got married and enjoyed riding together around

rural Pennsylvania or between State College and Philly, about two hundred miles. On Highway 32 after a series of hair-raising turns there is a prominent rock you might crash into in bad weather. When it's exactly in front of you, you can read "Are you prepared to meet your maker." One spring break we decided to ride to Vero Beach Florida 1,000 miles. We got a tent and sleeping bags hoping to camp on the way. We tried to set up camp on the edge of a freeway rest area, but North Carolina had different idea and a State Police Officer ran us out of the rest area. Motel that night, unbudgeted expense.

Six miles from Coosawhatchie, that's the real name, South Carolina the bike began to miss again. I pulled over to look for the obvious, nope everything was still connected. I kicked the starter and miraculously the bike started. We sputtered into town and found a little motel for the night. I thought maybe we could limp to a larger town in the morning. It would not restart cold even after I kicked 'th' bjesus' out of it. Since the right piston was new, I suspected the left one. With my experience I was able to pull the jug (cylinder and head assembly) easily. Sure enough, the piston was cracked just like the other one had been. Needless to say, there was no dealer in Coosawhatchie. We were lucky there was a motel, six rooms. I walked up and down the main street, about two blocks, asking for a shade-tree mechanic that is one who knows how to improvise when there are no parts. Maybe it could be welded; I had not yet discovered epoxy. There were apparently no mechanics of any kind. One person did offer to take us and the bike twenty miles to Savanna for $20, basically cab fare. He dropped us off at a decent motel.

There was no dealer or shop in Savanna that could help. I perused the phone books and found one in Jacksonville, Florida 140 miles. They had a second oversize piston for an R60, a miracle! I believe it was late on Friday and they would be closed until Tuesday, but I was able to arrange for them to ship the piston via Greyhound. That was how it was done before FedEx. It was going to take a few days though so using the city bus we got to know Savanna, a cosmopolitan city, pretty well. Many buildings had impressive wrought iron work that looked antique, but as it turns out was all made recently by a Harvard (or some other impressive school) drop out. He and his iron work were featured on 60 Minutes. Savanna had a lot of history, including being a pirate lair in the 18th century. We learned a lot about pirates, and sugar, their other industry.

I got the piston, but before I could install it, I had to remove something that fell in the engine. That required finding a magnet on a stick. The piston fit and the engine started up easily. The bottom end of that engine, that is the crankshaft, is really in the middle and is something you don't want to mess with.

We had lost a few days so we decided to settle for Daytona Beach instead of Vero. In those days you were allowed to drive on the beach, and I did, fast. It was fun 60mph on the place world records were made by people like Glen Curtis and Barney Oldfield. We swam in the ocean. I wanted to body surf, but the breakers were so far out that I kept thinking of sharks and came back in twice. It got late and I headed south on the beach back to the place we entered. Leaving the beach a little too fast or too slow, I hit soft sand that stopped the bike instantly throwing us both off, but no injury, just a broken mirror. Somehow, I missed the windshield.

We stopped at the dealer that had supplied the piston, but they did not have the identical OEM mirror that fit in the end of the handlebars. I settled for the generic mirror they had that went above the bars instead of extending out from the end. It gave a good view of my shoulder but not much behind. The staff praised the new four-cylinder Honda 500. Four cylinders in line offer a smoothness advantage because they have smaller pulses, evenly spaced and tiny pistons moving in opposition. Most small cars today are four-cylinder.

There are basically two ways to configure an in-line four. The less expensive and most common is a crankshaft with all the crank throws in one plane. Two pistons reach top dead center at the same time as the other two reach bottom dead center. Perfect secondary balance and the firings are every 180 degrees perfect primary but the pistons at TDC do not experience the same acceleration as the ones at BDC so there is some tertiary imbalance. Volkswagen, Subaru, and Honda Gold Wing flat fours reduce this with opposed cylinders. The other more expensive in line four has the crankpins offset 90 degrees so that only two pistons at a time pass dead center instead of all four. It makes a more expensive crankshaft. There are lots of more subtle variations. Today a lot of engines have a secondary balance shaft or even two and can run as smooth as turbine or an in line six. It looks like the inline six, and the V8 are being replaced by the V6. A V engine is like two in line engines that share the same crankshaft. Usually they are ninety degrees apart. It took 30 years to figure out how to make a V6 as smooth as an inline 6. The secret is staggered crankpins on the same throw. There are three cranks, but each has two crankpins, about 60 degrees apart. Machining it was quite a challenge. This made it possible to have the firing intervals evenly spaced, perfect primary balance. No two pistons pass dead center at the same time, excellent secondary balance and just a tiny wobble imbalance that can be fixed with counterweights or a balance shaft. The result is a very compact package that runs smoothly.

Equipped with two new pistons I felt confident and we headed home. We were not too lucky. The first day out we got caught in some serious rain on the freeway that I was not prepared for. At freeway speeds the raindrops hitting your fingers hurt. I don't know how anyone tolerates them on his face, yet some do! The bike began to miss again at Henderson North Carolina, a bit bigger than Coosawhatchie but not big enough to solve our problem. I waited for the bike to cool pulled the jug, at curbside. Some local bikers, with Japanese bikes, had come by; at first, they started to tease me the Yankee hippie on a funny looking bike, I just soldiered on. Soon one loaned me a wrench and they became helpful. We moved the bike to behind the police station. Small town blessing. I had pulled the jug again because I could and concluded not to make further attempts, just slipped it back on.

No sense in throwing another $100 piston at the engine until we figured out why they were failing. There was not enough time left on my break anyway.

Now there were several issues. I had to get back to school. We had to fix, the bike. Bus tickets were easy enough, but how to get the bike to Pennsylvania was more challenging.

Motorcycles were still outside the mainstream, like when no welder would work on a Honda, and there was no service to relocate bikes. If I could palletize it, it could be sent motor freight, but that would take too long to initiate, and was expensive; towing company, even more expensive. We even considered buying air tickets and trying to check it as baggage, not impossible, but nearly so. Called a home mover they said only as part of a shipment of household goods. Great I said we will just add a lamp or ashtray and they said 1000 pound minimum; at $1.00 a pound, too expensive.

It was a small town, and with the help of my new found friends I was able to leave the bike behind the police station. Try that in any city. We took the bus home. Next week we returned with my Volkswagen to collect the bike. That required driving through Washington DC always an adventure. Most American cities look like a checkerboard. DC was conceived by a Frenchman Pierre Charles L'Enfant and the plan looks like the web of a hallucinating spider, with arrows running through it. I do not think there is a true right-angle intersection anywhere. There are occasional traffic circles. A wrong turn could put you on the road back to Frederick Maryland, or an endless circle around The Capital. An hour wasted.

Moving a 550 pound bike 400 miles with a 1600 pound VW beetle may not seem doable, but I had done it with the Dream, for 10 miles. The R60, like the Dream, had a double leading link front end, only bigger called an Earls fork. The axle is ahead of the pivot on the rigid fork, the exact opposite of a caster on a shopping cart, a trailing link. The significant difference was the length of the links 3 inches on the Dream 12 inches on the R60. In both cases, with the front wheel removed the leading links would set right on the simple 1967 VW rear bumper. I chained them down, tied some guy ropes from the bumper to the steering head and taped TOW on the trunk. After listening to the comments and guffaws of the roadside self-appointed experts we were off. The bike towed like a high-quality trailer.

The R60 as its own trailer behind VW, note he large trunk.

BMW was the first motorcycle manufacturer to use telescoping forks. Theirs, with a male lower slider is called upside down today because most others have a female lower slider configuration, but in the fifties, BMW switched to the Earls which was more durable easy to machine and highly wobble resistant. The high wobble resistance also made the steering a little heavy but it never bothered me. Maybe if I raced. Then in the sixties they offered telescopic forks on one model, the R69US. With telescopic fork it would have been very difficult to tow a motorcycle behind a car. Telescopic forks have less un-sprung weigh which improves ride and handling, but they require a lot of precision machining and are easily damaged. Imagine attaching the ends of two vertical cylinders to a horizontal bumper bar. One bizarre but comforting characteristic of the Earls fork is that under heavy braking the front end rises. With telescopic forks it dips like a car.

We took the bike to Stan, left it there and went back to Penn State. When he got around to it, he informed me that the reason it was cracking pistons was that the heads were cracked. The heads were cracked because the head bolts had torqued to 125 foot pounds, about 5 times the correct torque, amazing that they had not stripped out of the cylinders, or broken. Torque, in case you are not familiar is twisting force, like opening a pickle jar. BMW used to supply an excellent set of tools with a new bike. I think you could do anything with it but rebuild the transmission. This set had one bent wrench. The exact size that fit the head bolts. That probably explained how it got to be bent.

Stan ordered two new heads from the factory and we waited, and waited. While I was waiting I asked around. I also wrote to BMW about my disappointment with the long wait for parts. I found a pair of used heads, a lot cheaper than new. The day I took delivery of the used heads I got a letter form BMW apologizing for the parts delay. They had just moved motorcycle production from Munich to Berlin. Because of my letter they said they were had restarted cylinder head production early. Where should they send them? I was already committed to the used heads, so I had to say thanks but no.

We had decided that since the heads were damaged the cylinders might be warped too. I had them bored out to 650 ccs and install appropriate larger pistons. The increase in power almost 10% was noticeable. After a while one of the spark plugs blew out of the cylinder head. OK a spark plug was only a dollar but it took the bronze insert with it. To prevent people stripping out the spark plug holes of an aluminum cylinder head a pre-threaded bronze insert was cast in. That part would be literally impossible to obtain so I had to find it. We combed a half acre field to find that plug. Fortunately, I did, unfortunately, I found out why I was able to find used heads. The insert was designed tapered like a dovetail joint, big end in. The inserts had blown out before. Someone had hammered them back in backwards like a cork in a test tube, then punched the metal around them to attempt to hold them in. Newer aluminum head engines use spark plugs with 50% longer threads instead; that works well. Spark plugs standards had been designed for older cylinder heads made of cast iron that is much harder than aluminum.

I consulted with Dr. Schmidt my metalworking professor about how I might secure them and he suggested high-temperature epoxy. I could only find one kind of epoxy. I turned the inserts the right way, buttered them with epoxy and hammered them back in. I took a hammer and punch to the heads to crimp the inserts in place also. Out of an abundance of caution I also epoxied a large washer over the inserts. That repair never failed. Unfortunately, the next failure was more serious. I was riding back to Penn State from Hatboro when all the idiot lights came on both of them and the bike started to shake violently. I had to shut it off. This was on the Pennsylvania Turnpike, but fortunately it was downhill to an off ramp and exit. We rolled it to a parking lot, found a phone and called my Dad. He and Mike showed up with Mike's 60 Dodge.

We stripped the luggage off the bike and put the whole 550 pound bike in the trunk. Try that with your Audi.

Mimi and I hitched a ride to Penn State and Mike took the bike back to Stan.

The crankshaft had been made in five pieces then pressed together. This allowed the use of more efficient roller bearings instead of plain bearings on the crankshaft. Either the extra torque or the months in storage with dirty oil were too much for it, the crank had twisted completely out of alignment so the crankpins were no longer in the same plane as the main bearings. It was not repairable and replacing the crank in that engine where the crankcase was cast in one piece was a huge job. It probably damaged the crankcase too.

A new crank was more than the bike was worth, or Stan had a used R50 engine that would fit but that also was more than good sense would allow. I let him keep the bike for his trouble. To add insult to injury a classmate with an insane-Kawasaki kept teasing me the BMWs were never reliable. The insane Kawasaki was a 500cc three-cylinder two stroke that could do a quarter mile from a standing start in under ten seconds, right out of the box, that is, with no tuning. It was competitive with purpose built drag race cars. They were not expected to last.

Two stroke, or two stroke cycle is an engine configuration you won't see much anymore. Almost all engines now are four stroke cycle. Suck, squeeze, bang, blow. First stroke the piston moves toward the crankshaft (bottom) and sucks in air and gas through the intake valve. The valve closes and the piston the cylinder moves the other way compressing the mixture. At the end of the compression stroke a spark ignites the mixture. Bang, a controlled explosion sends the piston back down converting heat to torque, mechanical energy. In Italy they call it an explosion engine to distinguish it from a diesel. At the bottom the exhaust valve opens and the piston rises excluding the spent heat and noise.

In a two stroke cycle the blow and suck happen near the bottom of the piston travel. The compression occurs in the crankcase as the piston descends. A port, hole, in the cylinder wall allow the compressed mixture to flow from the crankcase through the cylinder and push the exhaust out another port on the other side. Since you get power every revolution the power output is high, but since exhaust and intake happen at essentially the same time there is a loss of efficiency. These were the engines that required oil in the fuel so they smoked a lot. Some two stroke engines can have a separate blower to force the breathing.

I was motorcycle-less until Graduation, but for graduation my Dad bought me a brand-new set of Craftsman power tools. I still have them. They still work.

New Wheel a CB 350

1971 was a bad year for engineers to graduate; the space program was in the doldrums and the SST had been cancelled. Many of my classmates suddenly decided to go to graduate school, join the Peace Corps or try a different major. Because I was graduating in April though, I had a head start and I got an interview offer. The interview was at B&W, Babcock and Wilcox. People notice or even get confused by the similarity between B 'n W and BMW. There was a bad joke about B&W being the Cox Brothers, Bab and Will. My interview included a plant tour, and I think I fell in love. I enjoy big things and one of the first things I saw I thought they said was a submarine, and I wondered how that could be on the middle of Ohio. It wasn't, it was a steam generator for a nuclear power plant, but it looked big enough to be a submarine. It was about ten feet in diameter 100 feet long and weighs about 600 tons. Imagine a steel hot dog the size of a 737. Next to it was a reactor for a submarine somewhat smaller. I got the job offer in Plant Engineering, although my degree was industrial engineering. I don't think anything I did fit my IE courses.

Ohio was not my first choice of location, but as Dr. Schmidt said, they bake bread everywhere, you will be OK. I enjoyed the challenges of dealing with things big. I would see an ad for a tool then call and ask if they could make it ten times as big. One division liked to say we only do three things here. We cut metal, we weld metal and lift heavy objects, carefully! Heavy as in 600 tons. I wound up though in the heavy forging division. We took a 15-ton ingot of red- hot steel, poked a hole in it and then stretched it out to 30 feet long. We also took large steel plates 8 inches thick,

8 feet wide and 30 feet long, bent them into a half cylinder. Then we welded several of them plus an end dome together into a steam drum 5 feet in diameter and 150 feet long that weighed about 250 tons. In the assembled boiler it goes on the 30th floor level.

I found an apartment in Barberton, ten minutes from work, and bought a bike. I was impatient and did not want to shop, so I bought a new Honda CB350. I bought the bike with a sissy bar so Mimi could not fall off, but no luggage.

The adventure started right away. The salesman messed up the paperwork right after my wife left the dealership. To avoid calling her back, he forged her signature and the loan was approved. I got on the bike to ride it home and ran out of gas within sight of the dealership; they were that stingy.

I had a warranty claim the first day. The neutral light would not always come on when it should. Their answer, "You are not all the way into neutral," ignored the fact that it clicks into place.

My motorcycle adventures were less ambitious. I had it only a month when on a country highway a car turned right in front of me. I thought, "This is what it's like to die." I over-braked and the bike went down. I slid under the rear of the car with no contact. An eye witness thought there was contact and went after the driver. He caught the driver and brought him back to the scene. The witness turned out to be an insurance adjuster, for my own insurance company. The other driver acted indignant about the incident like somehow the whole thing was my fault. The bike damage was minimal, I had some torn clothing, but Mimi's hand would take several months to heal. The next day I went in a parking lot and practiced panic braking.

Mostly though, I rode it to and from work. Motorcycles were permitted to park right by the gate, but cars parked a half mile away. I even rode it in snow sometimes because I only lived about two miles away. After about a year I had a new draftsman assigned to assist me and he also had a bike, a CB360. At lunch time we would slip out and ride for a half hour or so even though the factory surroundings were less than scenic.

Mimi and I took day tours of the Akron area, but Ohio is mostly pretty flat fly over country and not as much fun as mountain states. Strangely though, Ohio had the highest per capita rate of motorcycle registrations in spite of the three-month layup season.

After a year of renting, we got claustrophobic and started looking for a house with some land and bought a 90-year-old house with a barn on 1 ½ acres for $20,400. It needed a lot of work, but I saw that as an investment. We liked to think of it as a farmhouse but it never really was.

One hears stories of superhuman strength in emergencies. I was doing chores in my barn my two kids Ali 6 and Steve 4 came in the barn to play. Before I could stop them, they climbed onto the Honda from the unsupported side. The bike of course toppled over on them. I grabbed the sissy bar with my left hand and flipped the 350-pound bike off them like it was a pillow. They were more scared than hurt.

I finally decided I needed luggage. I had seen scooters with a garbage can on the luggage rack but I was not prepared to go that low. Instead, I attached a number three mailbox to the sissy bar with U bolts. It worked pretty well for $12.

There is an amusing aside story. One day I walked into the shop, and saw a small poster everywhere with the headline $22,000 wrench. This was many years ago, so maybe add another zero. It had a picture of a very ordinary looking adjustable open-end Crescent® wrench. The caption explained that about a week before an employee confessed to his supervisor that he had dropped the wrench into an almost finished Navy aircraft carrier nuclear reactor. He considered not telling anyone, but after a few days the guilt finally got to him. The interior of the reactor looks a lot like a gigantic teapot full of spaghetti, but the spaghetti is stainless steel tubing. Except for a few hand holes, and two pipe connections it's all welded shut. By the way it, weighs 325 tons. It's shaped like a pipe tee with the ends capped. Now management had to decide what to do about it. Scrapping the vessel was not an option as it was worth many $million and due to be shipped. Leaving

86

the wrench inside was not safe. X-ray might reveal the wrench, It is very time consuming to x-ray through 12 inches of steel when you have access to both sides, but we only had access to the outside of the vessel. Then how do you get it out? How do you get one coin out of a piggy bank? They turned it upside down, that takes experienced riggers and two cranes. They listened, nothing. Suppose the employee was lying. Disgruntled union members have been known to set a red herring. The third time they inverted it they heard the wrench fall clink, clunk. After another 24 hours of turning it this way and that, the wrench fell out on the floor. Now all tools in final assembly bay have a lanyard tied to the user.

One day I was stuck behind a tanker truck that was waiting interminably to make a right turn. I noted that the driver was being extremely cautious about pulling out; maybe he knew how sluggish his truck was. Truckers are taught be patient, don't take a chance, there will be a break. I watched traffic and when I was confident the stream of traffic would make it impossible for the truck to move, I snuck between the truck and curb to get even with the front of the truck. When a gap big enough for a motorcycle occurred, as they always do, I went on my way. I scraped the curb a bit passing the truck. A few days later my work partner told someone else about this crazy rider who scraped the curb squeezing past a truck, but he did not identify me. He rode too, but a big Harley, which never would have been able to do what I did. I tried years later to contact him and learned that he had lost a leg in a motorcycle crash. He would not take the call.

Ohio is home to the two largest salt companies in America. I saw a film of the underground salt mine operation, using a big Caterpillar scraper like you might see excavating a new freeway. I'm not sure if this correlates, but Ohio does not plow snow. They salt it. They have plows, but nobody I knew ever saw them use one, just salt and more salt. Salt works OK if the temperature is close to 32 degrees F. It turns the snow into brine that rusts a car out in about 3 years. One day when it was close to zero, I turned in behind one of the salt trucks and the level road was too slippery to drive on. I tuned off up a secondary road that had not been salted and drove uphill with no difficulty. A lot of people keep a second winter-car to sacrifice to the rust god.

Another Ohio peculiarity. When a car is covered with snow or frost many people only clear enough off to be able to see straight ahead. In Pennsylvania we cleared all the snow off before driving.

Much of Ohio is cornfield flat. Ohio has a lot of railroad tracks, and almost all the crossings are at grade so when a train comes you wait. We were riding between cornfields and the way home crossed a single track. We arrived just a little after a locomotive crossed the road. Nothing to do but wait. As we waited the train went slower, and slower. One hundred and sixty- seven cars. Freight trains start and stop a little faster than glaciers. Slower, slower, stop. The last two cars still across the road. Then it backed-up.

We survived the Blizzard of 78, with a wind chill of 100 below zero and the lowest barometric pressure ever recorded inland. My barometer that B&W gave me for saving them a lot of money went so low the needle passed bottom dead center and started up the other side. We had so much snow that the next day there were cars in the trees, literally. Out of control cars hit the huge snow piles and came to rest 15 feet off the ground. It convinced me to move. I started interviewing for work in a warmer place.

I found a position in San Diego at Convair® division of General Dynamics®. Note I called it. Position not a job, read on, you will see why.

On reason I chose Convair® was Kaiser health care. No more insurance claim paperwork. They paid to move my household too, including the bike. We drove west towing our 17 foot Thistle sailboat, with three kids and two dogs in the trusty rusty '70 Ford van. We crossed a state a day and the kids learned which state came after which until Texas. "What comes after Texas?"

"More Texas"

"What comes after Texas?"

"More Texas"

"What comes after Texas?"

"More Texas"

"What comes after Texas?"

"More Texas"

"What comes after Texas?"

"More Texas"

After a few days in the Texas sun the dashboard that had been pristine, cracked all over.

That's one reason they test tires there.

Surprisingly, when you get that isolated the roadside restaurant food was excellent. Probably all local. We did not drive straight across, I detoured to Austin to visit my army buddy Jack. As you leave Austin you see what may be the world's most depressing road sign, "EL PASSO 527 MILES".

Do I have enough gas? Fortunately, there was gas in Fort Stockton. When we saw the first sign Welcome to San Diego Ali asked "Where's all the sand?" There was a running joke about Sandy Eggo.

Never heard of Convair? As of 1980 they had made more large airplanes than Boeing and McDonnel Douglass put together even though they had not built an airplane in 20 years. Of course, the definition of large has changed. Large in WWII was the B24, nicknamed "flying barn". It was bigger than the better publicized B17. The last airworthy B24 came to visit its home in San Diego. The B24 "flying barn" fuselage is smaller than the third engine nacelle of a DC10!

B24 was the most produced large airplane in history. In total about 24,000. Airplanes had been built one at a time like ships or hotels. The Army Air Corps wanted so many that they recruited Ford to mass produce parts. That still was not fast enough so Ford built an assembly line at Willow Run Michigan and in the last year of the war built 14000 of them.

Convair paid my moving expenses but the movers dented the gas tank of my bike. I started to make a damage claim and this is where the gotcha comes in. I applied to make a claim and was handed a nine-page form asking almost impossible detailed questions and making demands, like photographs of the bike before and after. Who photographs all their possessions before packing? It was not worth it for one cosmetic dent.

Convair had been bought out and dismantled by General Dynamics. We heard that the GD directors voted themselves a huge bonus if cash flow improved next year. Then they sold off half the assets to earn the bonus. The plant where I worked was the rump that was still called Convair. We made parts for the other aerospace companies. GD paid well and asked little. My friend Rich and I would ride our motorcycles down to the Embarcadero for lunch, nobody noticed if we came back late, or left early, or walked over to GD Electronics for a three-hour coffee break, or found an empty office and read for an hour. I once rode to the beach and back within the lunch hour just to prove that if I went to the beach and said it was on lunch hour it was possible. I brought back fresh seaweed for proof. I could just as easily have taken all morning and sometimes I did. It was unbelievably badly managed. Office supplies were rationed like narcotics, but engineering time was wasted regularly. We believed it was just some sort of welfare program. To solve their production problems, they brought in efficiency consultants from, wait for it, England. The modern country with the worst possible reputation for manufacturing inefficiency. Most of the British manufacturing had gone bankrupt by then. Most of their famous brands, like Triumph and Jaguar were out of business or bought out. The British industries had gotten so complacent that they would not improve a product that was selling because why bother if it's selling. If the product was not selling, well there's no money for improvement.

We had a secretary we nicknamed White Out Mary. By the time she was done fixing the mistakes in a document the paper surface was 60% Whiteout®. You had to be careful not to bend the original or it would crack and flake off. To proofread her work when you thought it might finally be done it was necessary to read it backwards one word at a time or you would miss something that White out couldn't fix, so it would have to be typed all over.

Most of the time engineers wrote a report long-hand, then sent the draft to Word Processing to be typed. Then check it and sent back for approval sometimes several times, with each iteration taking up to a week. We never understood why Word Processing was a separate department. Come to think of it, everything was a separate department.

I tried hard to be useful at first, but accomplished little. After two months I had a performance review. I was told I had not been there long enough for the review procedure, so no raise, even though I had documentation that in my first six months I had saved them $4 million, one hundred times my salary for the year. For the next six months I did virtually nothing, see above. Second performance review I got the biggest raise of my life 22%. I thought, well if that is what you want, I can deliver. That's why I call it a position.

My bike needed a chain, Rich's bike needed a chain. The chain was about $80 at the Honda dealer. It looked as far as I could tell like a standard Number 50 industrial chain. Each bike needed five feet. I called around and found a ten-foot chain in the factory box for $50. The shop was in El Cajon and had short hours. They were open Saturdays until 11:59 "If you get here at 12, the door will be locked" I got there at 11. The only problem was that the weight of ten feet of chain in my luggage mailbox made the handling poor until I relocated it to the very bottom. This important lesson came back to me many times. On two wheels, concentrate the weight near the center.

I started scheduling meetings at 4:59 or 8:59 and people were all there on time.

It seemed like I could ride to work 360 days a year in San Diego but occasionally it would rain and I did not like to arrive wet. I needed a windshield; found one at a garage sale. People warned me it would slow the bike down, but I went on with the project. I had to cobble up some brackets but I got it to fit. Now here is the surprise. It made the bike a little faster. Or at least quicker. It accelerated better as if it had more power. That may seem strange, but if you study a little aerodynamics, you learn that a flat plate has the worst drag coefficient, that is most resistance. The frontal area is large compared to the length. Two flat plates cause the airflow to behave as if the two plates formed a cylinder and reduce the drag coefficient. A pickup truck has less drag with the tailgate up than with it down (according to Chevrolet) for the same reason. The object with the lowest, slipperiest, drag coefficient is a mile-long freight train. The frontal area is 0.00001 compared to the length.

One day I thought the clutch lever had repositioned itself and tried to turn the bracket on the handlebar. Instead of moving though, it broke. It had been pinned in place to prevent rotation. That's when I felt really stupid because it had happened before. I should have known better. I remembered that, back at B&W I just put the part in my pocket walked it into the B&W Weld School and someone welded the very thin aluminum together, good as or maybe better than new. I think B&W encouraged things like that to challenge the instructors. We were told they were the best in the world according to the US Navy. A lot of legends went with the relationship. In WWII 80% of the US Navy ships had B&W boilers. Although the nuclear reactors were designed by GE, Westinghouse or Allis Chalmers we were told that the Navy insisted that all pressure vessels be fabricated at B&W. I did not have the welding option this time, but I did have the epoxy option and it worked as long as I had the bike.

One of the perquisites that went with working in maintenance at B&W was that small items like maybe an O-ring or Allen wrench that could be found in abundance. Taking one home for a 'government job' was not really proscribed. Allen wrenches were issued by the pound! Convair was the opposite extreme. Although management was unbelievably sloppy, petty supplies were guarded like gold. A secretary told me her husband was fired for leaving the plant with a pencil stub in his pocket. On the other hand, I borrowed a $100 reamer, half the size on a ball bat, took it home and brought it back with no issue. When I began work there, I was assigned a desk, and issued one pencil. When I requested a pad of paper, I was questioned how many sheets, do you really need the whole pad? If I tried to find a common hardware item like an O-ring I was asked "What does it fit?" I have bought my own assortment of 100 common O- rings in case I or a neighbor need one. It cost five bucks and I have been drawing from it for ten years. One O-ring in a package cost at least 50cents.

The tedium could be interrupted by extreme stress. One of the eight unions in that plant was threatening a strike. All salaried employees were instructed to show up for work Monday carrying a toolbox with a hammer and a pair of pliers, as if office workers armed thus could operate sophisticated numerically controlled machines tools and build airplanes. I'm not sure how I would handle that, but crossing a picket line on a bike was not my ideal. Fortunately, it settled. Having that many unions in one plant looks to me like a major management failure. Each union can go on strike pitting the other seven against themselves and management. GD probably thought it made corporate position stronger but it led to a lot of work stoppages.

Back at B&W where there was only one union, we had a gentleman's strike every three years. The workers would paint their houses, the office workers would get caught up on paper work and after 3 weeks the union would accept the company offer and go back to work. Delivery schedules were planned far in advance and there was no real disruption of business or careers. In eight years, there was not one unscheduled work stoppage. If there was a dispute as to who should have done some little task, the company just paid both workers and kept working. One time though we had to ship a 600 ton boiler drum while the workers were on strike. The railroad workers would not cross the picket line. Operating the in-plant locomotive was a union job. Management organized 100 office workers to push the railroad car far enough for the railroad to hook it up without crossing the picket line. Pushing railroad cars manually was not in any union job description.

I started yearning for a bike with longer legs. I started by looking at the bikes around me. There was an old BMW chained to the seawall right next to San Diego Bay. Although it was constantly exposed to salt air it had no rust or corrosion and the vinyl seat although dusty, looked almost new. All the Japanese and other bikes in town even inland had rust, lots of rust, peeling vinyl, faded paint and stripped out Phillip's head screws. I also looked at lots of odometers. Some BMWs had big numbers other bikes did not. The average life expectancy of a motorcycle was about 34,000 miles, but for BMWs it was about 100,000.

Another thing I noticed about BMWs. When it rains, motorcycle traffic disappears, except for BMWs. The *beemerphiles* just put on their rain-suit and ride on.

The only other time I came close to serious injury with that CB350 was trying to put it in my van unassisted. I did not have an adequate ramp, like a 10-foot 2x10, so I tried to do it with two 8-foot 1x6. The boards slipped and the bike fell, but not on me. I got it home some other way.

I asked $350 for the CB350 with over 20,000 miles on it. The buyer was so excited after a test ride I thought he would tear the pocket off his jeans getting the cash out.

ANOTHER BEEMER

I could buy a brand new three cylinder 750 Yamaha for less than a used comparable BMW. San Diego had several multi-line motorcycle dealers and Brattin® "Exclusively BMW" Motors, sort of a general store atmosphere where everyone knew everyone. I inspected parked motorcycles all over San Diego. Few had over 20,000 miles, except BMWs. Some BMWs were on their second 100k and had no sign of deterioration. Like the one chained to the seawall. No rust, no faded paint no peeling vinyl. Japanese bikes anywhere near the sea were thoroughly rusted. I decided to find a used Beemer and I found a lovingly cared for 1,000cc R100 with a frame mounted fairing, Krauser® bags and a trunk. About as equipped as bike came in those days before stereo, cell phone and GPS. I think it had 20,000 miles on it.

Mimi got impatient with the purchase procedure, or maybe she wanted me to sleep on it, but I had to come back the next day to actually buy it. People selling motorcycles are not so willing to let you have much of a test ride. They are afraid (with good reason) that you will crash and damage something of theirs. A rider on a newly acquired motorcycle is 60 times as likely to crash on the first day as the 200th day. (Hurt report data)

The seller was an obviously successful business man and I bought it largely on confidence. I entered the freeway, punched the throttle and whew, I was going 70 in first. That bike was a different universe than my past experience. We had one other industrial engineer who was very status conscious. He saw my new ride and told me I sure had class when it came to motorcycles.

Some days on the way to work I would sneak off for a ride

in east-county. I even tried the bike off road on an unimproved mountain trail. I could show up an hour late and wander around the factory for a while before appearing in our office. No one noticed, since most of the time I had no specific assignment. I even took it off road on BMX trails. It was surprisingly agile. I noticed though that after a while the access to the trails became motorcycle unfriendly, or should I say more challenging.

There are several Convair plants in San Diego and sometimes I would be given an assignment at another. GD had no compunction about causing the hardship to an employee of suddenly having to commute longer distances. GD has been described as the most efficient machine ever devised for removing money from the United States treasury, or some kind of welfare plan.

There was an incredibly inconvenient shuttle between the plants. Since there was a shuttle, they could require employees to commute from one to the other and not be reimbursed for travel. If one used the shuttle, it wasted most of the day, but no one accused GD of being cost conscious, just stingy. I just rode my bike. Twenty minutes as needed versus forty minutes oncean hour. Having a motorcycle again meant parking right by, actually under, the plant gatehouse. People often tease riders about; what if it rains? One rainy day the guys with cars laughed at me on the bike when we attended a meeting at the Kearney Mesa Plant across town. I rode others drove. At both ends I parked 50 yards from the door, they parked in the north 40. I had my Dry Rider suit with me and was parked near the lobby. It poured. I was the first to arrive back at base, walked in with my rain gear on. Stripped it off and was ready to go on break 20 minutes before the next guy showed up soaked from the 10-minute walks between parking and doorway.

Not only was I the first one back, I was the dry one who did not have to hike a quarter mile in the downpour through the knee-deep puddles. San Diego, like most of California is not equipped to handle more than an inch of rain in the same month.

An example of their penny-wise pound-foolish ways. As I languished half a day for an appointment in another department, I overheard another debate for hours at $15 an hour who would pay for a $10-part one time.

I did most of the routine BMW maintenance myself. I learned over the years to appreciate the parts man Blair at Brattin®. I lived closer to Fun Bike Center but when it came to parts their counterman did not know a fuel filter from a spark plug. Sometimes after ten minutes of fruitless search they would say "I'll have to call BMW" meaning Brattin, then find the part under the counter. It was faster to ride across town to Brattin, describe an obscure part to Blair and wait a whole minute for him to walk to the back and come out with it, like he had just found the same one for the previous customer.

Fun Bike was just around the corner but every time I gave them a chance to please me I wound up unhappy. They would tell me I needed new carburetors so I'd go to Brattin and they would tell me just to change a filter. My routine became change the oil and filter after six months. Take it to Brattin for a new rear tire and tune up once a year plus a front tire every other year.

I felt I owed GD two years for moving me from Ohio, they only demanded one. I was supposed to be an industrial engineer but the activity we spent most time on we called the Convair Shuffle. To actually have something approved to be done required the signature of the head of each affected department, and there were a lot of departments, not just the one making the part. Some departments would not sign off until a certain other did. The only way to get it done was to walk it through from one end of the mile-long plant to the other in a particular order that seemed to alternate ends of the plant.

They had a production control system that was color coded. If a job was on schedule the planning instructions were in a green envelope. If it was getting critical the envelope was changed to yellow. Behind schedule red. Almost all I ever saw was red. Part of the problem, a small part was a computer system called FASS, typical of Convair nobody knew what the letters stood for. We all knew that the wait time for a response from FASS was measured in lifetimes. Cartoons of a skeleton sitting at a computer terminal were everywhere. One of the flaws with FASS was that when you hit send, nothing happened. Inevitably after waiting way too long, you would wonder if you forgot to hit send and hit it again. Multiply that by 5000 employees, spelled "employes" at GD. One time I got an instant response "input ignored."

I had an hourly employee submit a suggestion that the FASS indicate input received in some way, but I don't think the suggestion was accepted. I could have done it myself, but she was eligible for compensation for suggestions and I was not.

There was also a quality control problem. The 'crib' where off specification parts were held for resolution had grown to a warehouse. I was asked to solve it. Sixty percent of the parts in a batch might be out of spec. The defects were not caught by the inspectors, they were caught at assembly when the parts could not be forced to fit. I put a sign on my desk. *"Convair quality, if it fits it flies"*. My boss made me take it down. Some of the defects were so obvious a child could see them. Some parts were ordered in pairs, half right hand and half left hand, but the batch might be two thirds left hand.

I also had a machine chip on my desk. It was cut from steel with a 30-horsepower machine. It was a number 6 chip about the size of my finger weight about 2 ounces. Beside it I had an aluminum chip from a 30-horsepower machine at Convair, it looked like a fingernail and probably weighed a gram, tops. The machine shop insisted that that was all the machine could do. They had big Cinncinnati® milling machines that you might see in an Army Tank Factory making tiny parts. A new engineer looked at what they were doing and asked "Where are the Bridgeports." Bridgeport® is great startup machine that your neighbor might have in his garage.

Just one more Convair story, although I have dozens. There was a tiny door spacer in the DC10, 24 per plane. It was the size of a quarter, but not as precise. It looked like a slice of white bread with two holes in it. They cost $25 each the Convair way. I made a simple change in the process and got the cost down to $15. Not satisfied with that I had the purchasing department put it out for bids. The bid price came in at $80 a thousand, yes you read that right, $80 a thousand. I took the proposal to the program manager expecting to be congratulated, instead the answer I got was "We don't need a thousand." I suggested buying a thousand and putting them in inventory. "No, we can only buy or make what we need for the current contract." How about buying a thousand and throwing away the extra ones? "No, we can't do that." I could not find a way to have the vendor make a thousand and just ship and invoice 24. I could write this same story about 4 times for different parts with the same answers. "No, we can't do that." Even if they had orders for ten planes, they would only make or order parts for one at a time. The final answer I got to money saving subcontracting was never mind the customer, "That don't make money for Convair." That's right the customer is us.

Government contracts used to be cost-plus that is cost, plus a percentage of cost. That was widely abused because there was no incentive to lower cost. After the war contracts went to cost plus fixed fee. That is a little better. Cost can include hidden profit, like buying a $100,000 Cincinnati where a $5,000 Bridgeport would be more efficient. Then keeping the use of them for decades. They also persist in inefficient methods that have room for skimming.

The money was good, but the boredom was overwhelming. Sometimes I would wander into an empty office and read magazines, come to think of it I might sit at my desk and read magazines. Once in a while I would get a real assignment something that on the GD schedule should take three weeks. I'd be done the same day. There were a few projects that kept me usefully in the plant, but not often.

I started looking for opportunities. Unfortunately, there were not a lot of well-paid openings that year for engineers in San Diego. I found an ad that said "auto experience necessary". I had automation experience so I called. It meant automotive experience, but John Fiske Brown still felt I was the most qualified. It was not a regular job though. I would be a subcontractor to a consultant in Forensic Engineering, specifically traffic accident reconstruction including motorcycle accidents.

It's time to pause here and define a few words that are often misunderstood. Engineer is a professional who figures out how to make things. Rocket scientists are really rocket engineers. In the past engineers also operated the war machines they built, so people who operate complex things, like locomotives or power plants are also called engineers. People who fix things are technicians.

Forensic does not mean having to do with dead bodies. It is Greek for debate and means work prepared with the understanding it is to be presented in court.

I was going out on my own. It started part time. For the first weeks I remained at Convair while assisting and learning, evenings and weekends. Convair gave us a week off with pay at Christmas so I waited until I got that check to turn in my notice.

I would be a consultant. And if good at it become a forensic expert. I had money coming to me out of the profit sharing, so I could do without a few paychecks. It seemed like $100 an hour instead of $2000 a month was worth a gamble. Things were lean at first, but on the other hand I had a lot of time to explore. San Diego County had thousands of miles of two-lane- blacktop. John Fiske Brown and I published a chapter in a book, then a book of our own then a book of my own and before I knew it, I was joking that if consulting is feast or famine, I'm ready for some famine. My first book, Motorcycle Accident Reconstruction, Understanding Motorcycles* was my publisher, Lawyers and Judges, fastest selling title. I once estimated that I had given a thousand depositions, but I was wrong 500 is closer, that's still a lot; I was doing one a week for years. A deposition can be intimidating. I think I was pretty good at it because my clients did not need to defend me. One would actually take a nap on the floor. Deposed can mean: exposed as a liar (legal system), or: removed from power (politics). Lawyers advise deponents not to volunteer anything, but I found that sometimes I could volunteer something that would drive the other side nuts. Or make them work really hard at it. Several lawyers asked me to cite each and every fact that supported my opinions. Since I had my files arranged so everything was in chronological order. I just started reading from page one, and by page three they were asking me something else.

Consulting meant lots of travel. You know, "A consultant is someone a hundred miles from home with a briefcase; who borrows your watch and tells you the time." We billed for travel time but I always tried to keep it to a minimum. On the big Beemer I could make it to the assigned location faster than anyone in a car. On the way back though, I would take long cuts, but still only bill for the shorter time. I discovered many a unique place. Sometimes it was something I wanted to go back to for a whole day. Southern California is a strange place. It seemed like you could take a country road in the morning and there would be a new shopping center the same afternoon.

When there was just one traffic light in Rancho California and it was a separate place from Temecula. You could take the one country road west and 90 miles later end up in Escondido only 20 miles away after passing through multiple villages that are not even on the map. On side trips like that I discovered Elfin Forest and Harmony Grove. I even considered buying a house in Harmony Grove. The house had its own bridge across Escondido creek, cool. I liked the name, but later found out there was so much squabbling they nicknamed it Disharmony Grove.

That bike was extremely stable. I can only recall dropping it once. I was on a slippery dirt road and a car came in the other direction taking my half. When I chopped the throttle, the rear slid out dropped me on the left side and I pitched over the bars. I broke the windshield and my left wrist, my first significant injury on a motorcycle. The next day my wrist still hurt, a lot. So, I went to the ER, got it X-rayed and casted. The cast technician complained that half his work was motorcycles. I told him he should be happy about that because otherwise one of the two of them would be unemployed. They thought about it for a minute and saw the point. By the way, watching them work was amazing. Viewing the bone through fluoroscope they can manipulate the break into perfect alignment then cast it so it heals better than new. Broken bones add extra mass when they heal. Doing nothing else made the technicians really good at it.

As stable as the R100 was there was one thing that scared me. Interstate 5 in LA county had a location where they restriped the road to gain a lane. (Went from 4 lanes at 14 feet to 5 at 11 feet.) There were joints in the concrete on overpasses that originally were between lanes. With the new alignment one was in the left tire track. Most riders know that the left tire track is the safest place to be in terms of traction and visibility. That joint however was about as treacherous as the trolley tracks on Baltimore Avenue. At 75 mph instead of 25 the wobble does not last long, but the adrenaline does.

Lots of travel involved tedium. I decided I wanted music so I bought an 8 track and cut a hole in the fairing for it. I had lots of 8 track tapes and the cartridges were more reliable that cassettes that have very narrow tape. This was way before CD or MP3. Remember all the discarded cassettes on the freeways, or drivers trying to rewind then while driving? Now they claim cell phones are too distracting. Unfortunately, only one of my cartridges overcame the ambient noise very well so I must have listened to that one a thousand times. I used small speakers in my helmet, technically illegal, maybe. The law said, "directly into the ear". The speaker was millimeters away.

As I got more involved in reconstruction, I learned more about motorcycles and cars. John taught me a lot and since I was already an engineer it did not take too long for me to rise from his assistant to being qualified on my own as an expert witness, especially after we jointly published the article about motorcycle accident reconstruction. The legal definition is not the same as the public concept. A legal expert knows more than most people and can assist the trier of fact. A person with limited formal education can be an expert on his job.

A lawyer told me a trial story where his expert was a lineman, high school graduate. The plaintiff trying to recover a kite had climbed a utility pole. He made contact with a splice in a high voltage (3000v) power line and electrocuted himself. His heart stopped, he fell and was dead before he hit the ground. The impact restarted his heart. He was revived and eventually recovered with some chronic problems. The lineman testified all day about his 40years- experience, then was asked only one question. "What do you think of that splice?"

"Worst splice I ever saw." Since that was all he said there was nothing to cross examine.

A legal expert does not need a PhD, just unique knowledge.

One of the most confusing things to laymen about motorcycles is steering. I knew from my early experience that motorcycle steering was not the same as most people's conception. Steering a motorcycle is as different from steering a car as steering a unicycle is from steering a bicycle. The steering is dynamic and integrated with the balance so it is in many ways more difficult and more critical.

Steering a car is a first order input. It goes where you point the front wheels and the front wheel angle is proportional to the steering wheel angle. Most of the time. Steering a two- wheeler above walking speed is a third order input. The input is not the amount of steering, but the force applied. Some call it pressure. The first response is not the change in direction, but the gyroscopic reaction of the front wheel to precess and lean. This causes the frame of the bike to lean also, and of course the rear wheel too. A leaning wheel becomes functionally a cone and a cone rolls in a circle. The amount of lean determines the radius of the circle. If the rider continues the force on the bars the angle will increase until it upsets. Fortunately, most of us learn to do it intuitively, until there is an emergency and a more powerful input we call counter-steering, aggressively applying the force that causes the lean.

This came to me when I met and worked with Luke. Luke was one of, maybe the first to teach motorcycle riding safety. He set up many programs, including bicycle safety for elementary school children and a motorcycle police force for Cairo Egypt. I never went wrong with Luke's advice. If it could be done with a motorcycle Luke had done it. I once mentioned to him that I heard of an outlaw biker who laid down his Harley to slide under a 40-foot trailer roadblock, then still sliding at about 40 mph got it back up and rode away. Luke calmly offered to teach me how to do it, but I do not think I'm that coordinated.

Luke was a career California Highway Patrol (CHP) officer and so soft spoken it was hard to picture him as a cop.

For a balanced motorcycle to travel in a curved path above walking speed there is no option but to lean. Some non-riders may think it's just for thrills. The lean angle is mathematically related to the radius of the turn and the speed of the bike.

Since you asked; Specifically, the mathematical tangent of the lean angle equals the ratio of the centrifugal force (or centripetal acceleration if you are a physicist and prefer that term) to the force of gravity (weight). That equals the lateral acceleration in g's, which might equal, but not exceed, the friction coefficient as with any other vehicle. If the ratio exceeds the coefficient of friction the bike is close to out of control.

The actual radius is even larger than the altitude of the cone shaped portion of the tires, in part because the tire develops maximum traction at about 30 percent slip and because the cone is an imaginary one formed by the tire contact points and a centerline projected from the axles.

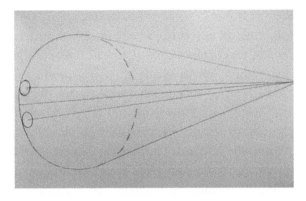

The two tire contact patches of a leaning motorcycle tire
describe the base of a large cone.

Friction coefficient is a basis for much controversy between professionals. You were probably taught that friction is simply the ratio between the weight and the horizontal force to cause sliding and is independent of area, period. What is often left out is "…if there is no deformation." Outside the physics classroom there is almost always deformation. Then there is the difference between static friction, like when you first try to push a chair back from the table, and dynamic friction like tire squealing around a curve. Static friction is pretty simple, if there is no deformation, but the difference where there is deformation can be dramatic, tile floor versus carpet. Notice that that analogy goes both ways depending on area. It is harder to push back your chair on carpet, but easier to slide a heavy box on a smooth floor if you put a piece of carpet under the box.

Dynamic friction can also be dependent on speed, and time. As the material heats from friction the coefficient changes. At drag races the first step before racing is called a burnout; deliberately spinning the powered wheels to heat up the rubber. It is so not-simple that articles, papers and books have been written about it. I read some and wrote some.

I spent a week in Charleston, South Carolina to rebut a physicist about that simple concept. The plaintiff had slipped on a shiny floor.

The plaintiff: a 56-year-old female, ex-tri-athlete, primary school teacher. She has had a weird tragicomic past; childhood sexual abuse by her father, homecoming queen, alcoholism, Olympic hopes, suicide attempts, college scholarships, two divorces, college diving coach, hospitalization for mental illness. Her father called her on the phone to tell her he was going to blow his brains out, then did it while she listened. Supposedly, once attractive, she has let her appearance go to hell, gray hair grown out halfway. She wears I'll fitting rumpled clothes, no makeup, and a grumpy expression. It is rumored that in six years she has aged 20, and she does look at least 70 at trial. Plaintiff claims her lifestyle has deteriorated due to the incident. She makes herself out as a happy well-adjusted citizen whose idyllic life of teaching, athletics, and coaching was abruptly halted by the incident. She required a partial hip replacement. The incident has left her broken in body and in spirit. It is not clear, from her rambling testimony, whether the incident contributed to her second divorce, or if the divorce came first. Come to think of it, nothing is clear from her rambling testimony. She was unhappy with her recovery after the partial hip replacement, so she elected a full hip replacement. Now she is depressed by the larger scar.

The only defendant was my client, a janitorial service contractor. They wax the floors and take out the trash work everybody wants done, but nobody wants to do. They employ the barely employable.

The incident: Early one morning the plaintiff slipped and fell on a shiny waxed floor at the school where she worked. She suffered a broken hip. Three witnesses recall that a child had vomited at the "exact spot", the day before, and that the school's day janitor had cleaned it up. The "exact spot" is a place located somewhere between 5 feet and 100 feet from the water fountain. All three eyewitnesses are fellow female elementary school teachers. They all testify that the school floors were always shiny, wet looking and *"sleeck as aice"* South Carolina accent. They all slipped too, although in different parts of the building in different months. None of these slips, on this slick as ice floor were ever reported. Plaintiff testifies that she remembers thinking that she must have slipped on the "leftover vomit". The witnesses however, all say it had been cleaned up.

The legal basis: She could not legally sue her employer, (workers compensation exemption) so she sued the janitorial contractor. The janitorial contract called for a "wet look" on the floor. She sued for one million dollars. The basis for liability was that the floor was shiny, therefore dangerous.

The plaintiffs Slip and Fall Expert: An Electrical Engineer and Contractor tested a different shiny floor. He had a floor specimen constructed that he thought was the same as the one in question and had it polished with the same products by a person who said he did it the same way as the defendant's employee. He concluded that this proved the school's floor was dangerously slippery. He did not even know how the school floor was constructed. The expert said he based his method and opinion on the book my partner and I co-wrote years ago. The defense called me to ask if I agreed with the expert's methods, results and opinions, I vehemently disagreed and was therefore retained to examine his work. When I still disagreed with his finding, I was asked to testify in the trial.

The Trial: Sitting in court is usually boring, but this was a soap opera.

Plaintiff's Lawyer: He has not tried a case in eight years. Constantly irritates the judge, late, confused, out of order, unprepared, runs out of witnesses, asks for favors out of "fairness". He does not know the law, or the protocol, but looks like Christopher Reeves, before the horse incident.

Defense Lawyer: could be played by Rick Moranis, in a $900 suit but he knows the law, knows the facts, knows the procedure, plays the judge like a violin and forgets nothing.

Plaintiff's testimony: Her replies are inappropriate, disjointed, rambling and incredible. At least 4 jurors and at one point the judge, are unable to contain their laughter. She will begin a sentence about a day at school, and end up at the Mayo clinic four years later. "Before school the day I slipped, I said to Millie... She is a redhead like... her hair is so long... you know long hair really is a lot of work to shampoo... but I love the new herbal shampoo's... but herbal tea I can do without, they tried to get me to drink it at the Mayo clinic, but I said..." She says, "I like the principal, but he's a lousy one and won't stick up for the teachers."

Plaintiff insists, at trial, that she slipped on "leftover vomit." There is no record of her ever mentioning this before, and her witnesses say there was nothing on the floor, nothing.

Her Lawyer then tries to introduce a privileged letter she wrote to him to show that she did mention the vomit previously, (to him) but he only wants to introduce that part of the letter, because the rest of it shows a vendetta attitude against the principal and the school board, who of course cannot be sued.

Plaintiff claims that although the injury was recoverable it had brought on fibromyalgia and atypical bipolar personality. As you probably know, fibromyalgia is a mysterious syndrome. It was clear from her history that the bipolar behavior predated the incident. Plaintiff's medical experts were mostly noncommittal. "Well, I did say her fibromyalgia might be related, but you really should ask her neurologist." Her psychiatrist was as incredible as the plaintiff was.

Plaintiff's lawyer brought in a psychiatrist who confirmed everyone's fears about *psychobabbling* shrinks with fifty-word sentences full of tongue twisting buzz phrases like "suicidally auditory." I almost fell asleep, and when I caught myself, noticed the judge and half the jury nodding.

Plaintiff's slipperiness expert actually made a very good Mr. Wizard type presentation, he appeared to know what he was talking about, and explained it very well. He severely tempered his opinions when he learned that I was there to rebut him, but still clung to obsolete disproven notions about slipperiness. He says things are not slippery when dry, except ice and glass. Those actually are not slippery dry either, but in South Carolina they don't have much experience with ice outside of a glass. His methodology, pulling the plaintiff's shoe across a different floor, was nonsense and his "Scientific Basis" for his ultimate opinion was without foundation. In his opinion: since a coefficient of friction of 0.5 or more when measured in a laboratory, with a James Machine is "anti-slip" anything less, even if tested by his questionable means, is unreasonably dangerous. Dance floor and bowling alleys us special wax for a 0.3 coefficient of friction.

To buttress the electrical engineer's opinions a physicist also testifies. His specialty is micro-optics, and he has not thought about friction since he was a college freshman. Nevertheless, he smugly testifies that friction is simple. Weight divided by horizontal force, that's all there is to it (it's beneath him) and anyone can understand it.

When I finally got my chance to explain friction as understood by mechanical engineers, and all the things the plaintiff's experts were getting wrong, the jurors were the most engrossed I have ever seen. Clean, dry, shiny floors are almost never slippery, high school physics be dammed. Quality floor wax properly applied and dried actually increases the friction. Shiny floors are prone to slipperiness when wet. That's reality.

After closing arguments, the Judge ordered lunch for the Jury so they could begin deliberating immediately. They ate lunch and rendered a verdict in 35 minutes, 12-0 defense.

Counter-steering is the real way that you steer a bike. Push or pull the handlebars in the opposite direction of the intended turn. The bars seldom actually move a noticeable amount. I'm not sure they move at all. I wanted to instrument a bike to find out, but that was one of my ideas that never materialized. To maneuver a motorcycle abruptly, you push on one handlebar, and that is the way the bike will lean. The way it leans is the direction it will turn, until the handlebars are relaxed or pushed the other way. Skilled riders learn to use counter-steering to initiate rapid steering changes, instead of just leaning into a turn. They can even pull the outside handgrip as they push the handgrip on the inside causing an abrupt change in lean angle. When the bike is at the correct lean angle, they force it back. This makes emergency evasive maneuvers possible. Many motorcycle safety instructors consider emergency counter-steering the most important part of the course.

The two tire contact patches form a tiny part of a huge virtual cone, and a cone naturally rolls in a circular arc. The intuitive rider just correlates leaning with turning, the same intuition that works on skis or a toboggan.

Pardon the redundancy, but the concept can be hard to understand. Repetition helps. For a more detailed discussion see Motorcycle Accident Reconstruction, Understanding Motorcycles*

Steering is also affected by "out-tracking." Children learning to ride eventually pick it up after many trials and failures. I think training wheels are counterproductive because with them, one steers the bike like a lawnmower. They turn away from the fall and amplify the problem. I called out to Amy, "Turn the way you are falling." And the problem of turning away disappeared.

I disagreed with the idea that out-tracking is how a bike steers. To experiment I rode close along a line of raised pavement markers. When I pushed the bars to turn away it did not run over the markers so there was no out-tracking. At low speed it was possible to turn with or without out-tracking. Pull one bar to initiate out-tracking, or push gently to turn without. I also experimented with low speed out-tracking. I drove through parking lot puddles at minimum speed then turned by various techniques combining counter-steering and out-tracking. It was possible for the front tire to turn inside the rear, just like a 4 wheel, or out-track at the rider's discretion. At low speed both can occur, but at highway speed, i.e., anything over 14-15 mph counter-steering predominates and controls the bike.

The novice rider, in a panic, may revert to training wheel or tricycle experience to steer by only turning the handlebars in the direction he intends to turn. Physics will prevail over intent. He might wind up turning into the very thing he chose to avoid. Often, we heard the claim the handlebars locked up. My first experience was at age 15. I was riding very fast down a steep hill, with a sharp turn. It felt like the handlebars were frozen, but intuition let me steer by leaning, and I did not crash, for which I was grateful. I could have just as easily tried to steer like a tricycle and crashed. With counter steering a motorcycle is about as maneuverable as a car and does not need as much road to escape. Cars don't tip over easily and can deal with surface irregularities better. I did not learn that all at once. It started with my Honda dream or maybe my bicycle and progressed though many rides on different machines from a moped to a Gold Wing, to a dirt bike or crotch rocket and reading dozens of books, hundreds of magazines and countless depositions of victims, witnesses and other experts.

That BMW R100 had unique turn signal controls with a button on each grip to activate the signal for turning that way. The signal would come on instantly and then blink. I used that to video a 12-foot lane change in less than 1.4 seconds from input to alignment in the new lane. I initiated the maneuver by pressing the turn signal button hard. I used that bike to dispel another commonly cited constant. In accident reconstruction it is common to cite 1.5 seconds as the reaction time for a reasonable alert driver to apply the brakes in response to a simple stimulus. Some so-called experts claim that is inviolate. I was skeptical, because nothing biological is absolute, that's why mountain climbers say never trust vegetation. It is just an average. For traffic signal timing the conservative assumption is 4 seconds. We did an experiment. My partner John would start his stopwatch, when I heard the beep of the watch, I would apply the front brake. When he saw the tail light come on he would stop the watch. We did this over and over and never got more than 0.55 seconds for the total of both our reaction times and the system delay. So at least one of us had a reaction time of 0.275 second or less. Not 1.5 seconds.

In western action shooting there are some who can draw, aim and fire in less than 1.5 seconds from a signal. A pitcher can catch a line drive less than half a second after the crack of the bat.

I got in the habit, if I was having lunch alone of going into downtown Solana Beach (one of the smallest cities in California) then taking the long way back via little used rural roads. I used the same one over and over so I improved my confidence and ability to ride fast. How fast compared to as fast as possible, I don't know but I never crashed or got a ticket, but I was going about twice the speed limit. The worst thing that happened was coming around a bend and discovering too late a guy spray painting a fence. I had white dots on the bike forever. That bike along with my research taught me a lot. Luke told me not to worry about low-speed wobble that some people like to call speed wobble or tank slapper. A firm grip will damp it out, so will leaning into a turn, slowing down or even speeding up. I tried all of those things after deliberately inducing low speed wobble by letting go and hitting on end of the handlebar. The one thing that won't work is to try and fight it directly. No one's reflexes are that fast. If I read something about handling that intrigued me, I could go out and try it. For example, I tried braking until I got good enough with that bike that I could tell by the sound and feel when I was nearing lockup. Fortunately, that bike was so stable that even when I did lock up the front brake on spilled anti-freeze it did not go down.

It came with an alarm. I never really felt the need but I used it. The only time it sounded I was in deposition a half block away. I asked for a break and we all ran out to see. The woman, whose car was in the next stall, apologized for bumping my bike. I did have something stolen though and the alarm did not help. I had a Bart Simpson doll zip tied the luggage rack and someone cut the zip tie. I was too far away to have heard it.

Adverse weather is more concern on two wheels than four. If either wheel slips too much, you are probably going down. I crossed a shallow stream on one of my long cuts home and felt the front wheel slip and wobble momentarily. I wondered if I hydroplaned or was the bottom slimy. I parked the bike and went back to check; the bottom was slimy. I was extra cautious on wet roads, but did not think motorcycles tires could hydroplane. I eventually got a book called The Physics of Tire Traction. Reading the book and doing the math convinced me that hydroplaning of motorcycle tires is extremely unlikely. The motorcycle tire contact patch is more like a canoe than a hydroplane.

The more I got involved, in consulting the more things I began to carry with me. My camera bag grew to a briefcase that fit in the bags that came with the bike. They were Krauser® bags, highly respected. One day however the right bag flew open and I lost my briefcase that contained some valuable papers and my checkbook. After that I was careful to double lock. A year later the right bag, fortunately empty, flew off. Tumbling down the freeway at 60 mph it quickly disintegrated. It took a month to find one used one and not have to buy a complete set with brackets and all. After that I created a sling that went around both bags and kept them on and closed reliably but was little trouble. My camera kit kept getting bigger.# Remembering the chain in the mailbox I reluctantly moved my camera kit into the trunk it weighed more than BMW's recommended allowance.

> #Two camera bodies with speed winders and data backs Lenses, 4
> Flashes, 2
> Steel tapes: 100-foot; 35-foot, 2; surveyors 7-foot pocket rods, 2 Folding 8-foot carpenter's rules, 2
> Tripod and target
> Obenski Folding Photo-scales, my invention, 2
> Calipers, Vernier and Micrometer
> A few common tools Number cards Machinist rules
> Tape recorders, 2 or 3
> Film, dozen rolls, recording tape, several, spare A76 and AA batteries

Some things come as a complete surprise. Once, after my client won her case, she interviewed the jury. It seems like the deciding factor was that the jurors saw me arrive at the courthouse carrying a VCR on my motorcycle. This convinced them that I was sincere about my motorcycle expertise. It was not the biggest thing I ever carried on that bike. The biggest was a large pair of stereo speakers about 2 feet high.

Carrying my camera kit in the trunk did not work out well.

One day at about 80 mph I felt a high-speed weave. This is the scary one. If allowed to continue it will amplify and throw the rider off. There are three suggested ways to deal with it. Speeding up supposedly will change the frequency and make it go away, but you will have to slow down again and it might still be there. I rejected that one. Slow down, but very gradually, that might work if you can slow down gradually, quickly. I did not like that one very much either. I chose number three, move weight forward. I slid up on the seat until I was pressed against the windshield and the bike settled down. I kept my speed down that day.

I decided to move my camera kit further forward to improve weight distribution and never had the problem again. This made room in the trunk for some lightweight kit but I could not leave the bike unattended with thousands of dollars-worth of equipment bungeed on the seat.

I wanted to carry still more on the bike, so I bought a 24-inch tool box that I could place on the seat and attach to the luggage rack frame with extended shackle padlocks made to lock bicycles. I locked my camera kit in the box with a small padlock to keep the honest people out. The first time I used it for a crash site inspection, I forgot the key. My assistant Tyrone met me at the site, so I sent him to buy a hacksaw to cut off the lock. While he was gone I realized the box was plastic so instead of cutting the lock, I cut the plastic with my pocket knife and went to work. Now the box was no longer lockable, but all I had to do was epoxy a metal plate with a small hole over the new defect and the box was stronger than new. The luggage rack was not as sturdy as it could have been and the brackets made of rather thin steel tubing cracked. They were small parts that cost too much so I re-welded them more than once but they never failed catastrophically. My welding skill has never risen above entry level, welds that look awful, but sometimes seem to hold.

This was my first bike with tubeless tires. I remember the skepticism when tubeless tires were introduced for cars. They are a real blessing for bikes, because you don't have a spare, and finding the correct size tire or even close, is not easy. A set of tire plugs and a small electric tire pump will get you home. Most of the pumps look too big but if you take off the plastic housing the actual pump is smaller than a can of instant tire inflator. I also tried CO2 cartridges but it took too many to do the job. That bike had a hollow compartment behind the seat that held the tool set, tire pump, and folded up Dry Rider suit. The seat had a lock that required its own key, I found that a nuisance so I had a locksmith rekey the seat lock to use the same key as the ignition and fork lock. He did that by discarding a few tumbler pins, commenting that I was losing some security but I was not worried about someone stealing that which was under the seat. Most security is an illusion. A determined thief will almost always get something, but most theft results from opportunity. The presence of a lock is usually more than enough.

I was on my way to Del Rio Texas for a trial. I was seated in the plane with them about to close the door when the flight attendant came to me and said, "Mr. Obenski you don't have to go to Texas." What did that mean? If I stayed on the plane and the case was closed, I could be stuck for the airfare. If I did not go and the trial proceeded without me, I could get sued for damages.

I got off and ran to the nearest phone and called my office; the case had settled. The next week I bought a cell phone, The Brick. The case was metal, held together with screws. Being an engineer, I had to open it up and risk voiding the warranty. I don't know much about electronics, but one thing was obvious: that brick had more computing power than existed on the entire planet when I first learned the word computer at age 9. Then I tried to figure out how to integrate it with my bike. For those who do not remember, this was the first generation of hand- held cell phones. It was a little bigger than a common brick and just as square with an antenna that stuck out 6 inches. It had memory of 72 numbers, and a battery that had to be replaced twice a year. Even connected to external power it would not work with a bad battery. The reception ranged from poor to spotty. I figured out how to install it in the right glove compartment with the optional 12-inch antenna. Hands-free was still in the future, but I cobbled up a way to have an external mic and headphones. It was hardly worth having it but Pacific Bell was busily removing payphones. That made it difficult to check in with the office. They had lost a lawsuit by a guy who was in a phone booth and could not figure out how to open the door in an emergency. A year later the brick was stolen. I found a used one that would fit in with my system, but it did not work even as well as the first.

Why would I go to Del Rio Texas? There was a car there with an alleged defect that caused it to go out of control and turn over. I had gone to Del Rio, before, met with a mechanic there, found an anomaly in the transmission. Del Rio is three hours from the nearest commercial airport, San Antonio, so I had arranged a Cessna charter flight. The charter pilot with the best price was out of Del Rio. He made two round trips, one to pick me up and one to take me back. He was still the low bidder. The transmission went by FedEx later.

One day, after a fast ride I looked down and noticed that the cross bolt that helped retain the rear axle was missing. The axle is basically a big bolt with a nut on the end, but in case the nut comes loose they had a secondary pinch bolt to keep the axle in place, German engineering redundancy.

Riding fast is fun, but sometimes afterward you wish you had not, especially if it involves the police. Once I noticed a police motorcycle ahead of me with his saddlebag open at the top and all the contents at risk of blowing out. I wanted to catch up with him, but he kept speeding. Eventually I did. He thanked me for the help, then lectured me about speeding.

I have had other unusual encounters with police. I was assigned to inspect a vehicle in police custody but when I went to the cop house, they told me it was at a different location. The officer said just follow me. It was far enough that the route involved freeway. The officer was astute enough to keep his speed down. Unfortunately, cars kept passing me, but none would pass a police car. By the time we got to the off ramp for the storage yard there were twelve cars between us.

A different time I was sent to inspect a wreck in *Tecate* Mexico. As usual with assignments in Mexico there was no address and vague directions. Driving back and forth on the highway between Tecate and Guadalupe I noticed a Police car in a field with some wrecks so I turned in. I was a half hour late. The *Federale* had made everyone wait for me to arrive before allowing anyone to get near the car. Afterward, he had us all follow him to his station. A different officer indicated that we were all to follow him, I hoped to the crash scene. I was the last in line and he drove very fast. That would not have been a problem except for the second officer behind me. Was he the rear escort, or a patrol officer ready to give me a speeding ticket? Fortunately, the following officer turned off and I was able to catch up to my escort, at the crash scene. There was a Mexican law that forbade visitors to work in Mexico, but I experienced nothing but curtesy in spite of the language barrier. Come to think of it, in many trips to Mexico I have never had a bad experience with their law enforcement. It helps to be patient.

The EPA took leaded gas off the market. This bike had fairly high compression and with 500 cc per cylinder the lack of 100 octane gas made it knock. Bigger diameter cylinders are more prone to knocking; that is one reason to have a multitude of small ones. Changing the timing would help but the only real cure was to lower the compression. Fortunately, there was an easy way to do that on the boxer engine. Instead of modifying the cylinder heads or replacing the pistons one could add an extra base gasket under each cylinder. I had experience removing and replacing the jugs, but they had improved the exhaust pipe connection. Instead of two screws to disconnect the exhaust pipes there was a huge aluminum nut the size of the nut on a sink drain, but torqued tight. It had large aluminum fins and no provision for a wrench. To unscrew that you needed a special wrench that was $80 at the time, 1980. If you took the nut off without that wrench and damaged the nut you had to replace the nut and pipe, because the nut was captive on the pipe and cost about $200. I realized that if I took the mufflers off first, I could remove the jug with the exhaust pipe still attached. I did have to readjust the valve lash, but with the cylinder heads sticking out like stubby wings that job was as easy as valve adjustment gets. You can do it sitting upright on a stool. I felt the bike ran hot after that so I bought a special oil pan that held an extra quart and had more cooling fins and cooling tubes through it. That worked, but took away some ground clearance. The only other design improvement I made was a fork bridge to make the front end a little more wobble resistant but only because it was recommended not because I ever felt a need.

One great feature that took an emergency for me to really appreciate was the 8inch headlight. Car headlights were ether 7inch diameter or even smaller if there were 4. Not only did it do a great job of illumination but on the occasion when someone stole my right of way the high beam looked closer and got more respect. Maybe it looked like a locomotive. People respected it. The horn, though better than most motorcycle horns, was inadequate and I supplemented it with an electric air horn. There seems a quirk in the way horns are rated. Both an electric horn and an air horn will claim to be 120 decibels but the air horn will seem louder. I suspect the standard for air horns is decibels measured at 50 feet and the unrelated standard for electric horns is decibels measured at 6 feet or something like that. Standards are great, but often not unified.

One of the scariest things that ever happened to me was on that bike. I was on my way home from Riverside on the I 15 when my left eye switched off. It was totally dark and I started wondering what to do. What if the other went dark too? I thought about looking for a hospital. A few years before, at Convair®. Both eyes had switched off and left me totally blind for about a minute. Before I could ask anyone to check, they came back and I forgot about it. I have had ocular migraines (squiggly flashing lights on one side of my vision) all my life, but only got a valid diagnosis in the 80's. One Doc thought it was a form of epilepsy. It was as if no one else ever had the symptoms. I figured out in high school that the trigger for the events is bright light, but realized only in the 90's that the proximate cause in my case is sodium nitrate. I stopped eating certain lunchmeats and rarely have more attacks. I don't know if the two anomalies are related. On a motorhome trip in 2017, I had a *squigglies* attack, the first one in ten years. I realized that I had eaten the same brand of lunchmeat as caused the problem before. It is a form of migraine, but in my case no headache except right after a doctor questioned that I did not get headaches. I realized that the headaches were due to his suggestion, and never had one again. Four things seem to cause migraine, caffeine, sodium nitrate, chocolate and aged wine or cheese. I'm immune to the others.

I had a couple of flat tires with that bike. The center service stand was designed to lift the rear wheel but positioned so that if you removed the front wheel the bike would rebalance securely on rear. A flat usually meant re-inflate and hope to make it to a place where it could be fixed. More severe flats I could deal with removing the rear wheel, taking it to a service station and coaxing the people to plug a tire. Lots of them are afraid of the liability for a tire plug and will only repair a tire from the inside and their machines cannot do motorcycle wheels. One time I remember needing help to bring me something to repair a flat on the I 5 near home. Not only did the repair fail to hold, the tire unseated from the rim bead. There was nothing I could do with it. I ditched the bike on its side in the weeds, took the wheel with me to a motorcycle shop then back to bike the next day.

I often picked up kids from activities on that bike. My daughter Amy was so confident as a passenger she sometimes fell asleep. We were sending her to religious school and once she told me she would only go if on the bike and if I went a particular way so she could see the view. I also took her to a birthday party at Corvette Diner in San Diego and she got a greeting as if a rock star had dropped her off instead of only Pop.

About this time in my motorcycle life, we lost Mimi. I was suddenly a single parent but my youngest Amy was 13 so we coped. I was addicted to having a complete family so I engaged in some unusual behavior. One thing was taking the mufflers off my bike. The alternate firing design with a crossover pipe strategically located between the two exhaust pipes resulted in an amazingly not loud motorcycle. I could barely tell the difference.

I was not single as long as some people think one should be, but this wasn't the nineteenth century. At a Sadie Hawkins Dance I was instantly attracted to a tall woman at the newcomer table. The attraction was mutual and we were married before the year was out. It took me all of 30 seconds to convince her to ride with me also. Cindy and I are still in love 29 years later.

One day I stopped at a mini mart and when I put the bike on the center-stand; the stand broke and the bike toppled away from me onto a parked car. Broke my mirror and it might have scratched the car but the left side of the car war already totaled and rusted over so I ignored it. I parked the bike on the side stand. That weekend I took the center stand off and welded reinforcement straps on. It never broke again. Just to be safe I built a fixed stand in my garage to hold the bike upright with the weight on its tires.

I can't remember why I sold that bike. I'm pretty sure it had about 100 thousand miles on it. I did want a better sound system. As you can see most of my memories of it were pleasant, I remember taking a cat *Bohboh* to the vet on top of the tank bag. One night coming home late I had a different adventure with a cat on a local street. The cat ran out from the curb and right under my rear tire. We stopped and found an awake neighbor to tell so that the cat's owner could know, and we discretely disposed of the remains.

A LITTLE DIFFERENT

I traded the R100 for another Beemer, a K100 the radical, for BMW, version, a 4 cylinder. With the engine laid down lengthwise unlike other four-cylinder motorcycles.

The Boxer engine since the R32 has been intimately connected to BMW, unfortunately the design was getting uncompetitive to manufacture. Especially against the Honda Gold Wing 4 cylinder, later 6 cylinder opposed engine. BMW management considered getting out of the motorcycle business now that they were well established in the premium car business. According to legend thousands of loyal stockholders came out of the mountains to the annual meeting and threatened a revolution if they did. The result was the K Series and later the Oilhead® boxer twin.

I put a lot of miles on that bike in spite of the fact that my shoulder hurt almost the entire time I owned it. I even tried to find better handlebars. It was smooth and extremely reliable with a real stereo system that I hooked up to helmet speakers. Cell phones got better and I integrated the phone into the speaker system. That worked well enough that I once prepared for a deposition via cell phone while riding in serious LA freeway traffic. The K100 was also unique in having a single rear swing arm. This made changing the rear wheel as simple as it is on a car, actually simpler, no jack, just put the bike on the center stand take out three lug screws pull off either wheel. The bike would balance on the center stand and either tire. The brake rotor was another matter. I was unable to get one of the three flat head screws out. The Allen hex socket was very small relative to the thread diameter. I deferred that repair to the dealer. I realized later that I could have welded a nut onto the screw head. The heat cycle would loosen the screw and the bigger wrench would not strip. Otherwise, disc brakes keep getting easier to service.

I started getting more calls to test ride bikes for various reasons, two to verify that Harleys were repaired properly. I got paid to ride my bike 100 miles to the Harley shop, ride the Harley 100 miles then ride mine home. Tough job but someone, well you know. It is actually a scary proposition because if a defect could be found later I might be liable for not finding it. I think I was working for the defense at the time though, so they just wanted independent confirmation of their counterclaim. In my experience Harleys are easy to ride and BMWs are easy to ride fast. Seems like the old 55 mph national speed limit was made for Harleys because when the limit was 65 people rode Harleys at 55 and *Beemers* at 80 all day long. Other bikes went faster but seldom all day. The coast-to-coast speed record was held for about 40 years by a young man on an R69 with about 30-gallon gas tank capacity. Optional BMW 10 gallon, plus four Jerry cans plumbed in. This was before interstate highways were common.

One test ride involved as best I can remember a Honda R600R, a dual sport. The only bike I ever rode that would wheel stand on a punch, e.g., all I had to do to the lift the front wheel off the ground was open the throttle. That year I had about three cases involving that model.

While I'm on comparisons, we all know how loud they Harleys usually are but believe it or not they come from the factory as quiet as any Honda and HD makes a fortune selling replacement loud mufflers at $400 or more each. HD has an after-market chrome plated expensive replacement for every conceivable part of the product. There is a link from the shift pedal to the transmission. It looks like a screen door straightener, $4.95 at your local hardware store, $110.00 chrome plated. Add a logo to the turnbuckle in the middle $200 to sky's the limit. A Harley dealership is not like your typical motorcycle shop, it's more like Nordstrom's with bikes thrown in between chrome plated doodads and $6,000 couches with a Harley logo.

I have to give the HD organization credit. They have turned every negative comment about their product into an advertising success. Examples, a junkyard full of motorcycles with the caption: Can you spot the Harley Davidson in this picture? Neither can we. Harley simplicity and model longevity made it possible to rebuild them forever, like a Model A Ford. Another example a threatening group photo of the Hells Angels with the caption "Would you sell an unreliable motorcycle to these guys." At a "slave auction" fund raiser, men offered motorcycle rides to be purchased by women. Potential bidders asked the same question, "Is it a Harley®?" every single time. Harleys vibrate but some people find that particular vibration comforting. They have some newer models with the engine vibration isolated from the rider, but I'm not convinced that has helped sales.

Some people who object to helmet laws claim that helmets impair hearing. My experience is that by tempering the ambient noise they improve hearing sensitivity, just as sunglasses improve vision on a bright day. On Claremont Mesa Boulevard I began to accelerate hard not thinking about the speed limit, I was wearing what is called a full coverage helmet, that fits pretty tightly over the ears. I was able to distinguish the different exhaust sound of a KZ1000 police special behind me before I embarrassed myself.

Brattin® loaned me a BMW F650, like all *Beemers* quiet, but the air intake was located by my left knee so that when I punched the throttle, I got a mellow exhaust-note like sound that only I could hear. Two needs satisfied with one decision.

We bought a Honda Sabre for a test we never got to perform it had to do with a truck making a U turn in the bikes path. I think we were going to smash the bike to vindicate my calculations. The test never happened so the bike went back on the market. Before we let it go, I took it out just to have the experience even though there might have been a no-insurance issue.

I test drove a Honda Gold Wing aka *motorbago*. It's a huge 6-cylinder touring bike that has taken sales from Harley and BMW but also expanded the market. They are very popular. I did not care for the handling. The steering felt too light, like a moped but it weighs 600 pounds.

Another unusual test ride involved riding a Vespa over a speed hump to determine if a speed hump is more effective than a speed bump. Everyone is familiar with speed bumps they are similar to a three-inch pipe across the road. Crossing one is uncomfortable and the theory is everyone will slow down. In Mexico they are called *topes* and are more like a six-inch pipe. They work; slow down or need a tow truck. Impatient drivers learn that if you cross a three-inch speed bump at higher speed like 30, you barely notice. The vehicle suspension is designed to absorb that size irregularity. Speed humps were originally designed to work like a speed bump but not interfere with snow plows. Speed humps are about 4 inches high, but about 20 feet wide. It did not take long to discover that they are better than speed bumps because up to 15 mph they are barely noticeable but the faster you go the more annoying they are. The Vespa proved that, the speed hump was noticeable at 15 and frightening at 20 mph. You feel as if you might go airborne.

Vespa is the original motor-scooter. It was designed for transportation starved post war Italy. Italy's climate and narrow congested streets made it the perfect environment for a light small vehicle that got excellent gas mileage. Sales took off. Everyone who could, copied the concept.

From time to time, I was called upon to make a video from the motorcycle. On a hunch I bungeed a Sony Beta camera on a stack of egg cartons so it was looking through my windshield. The egg cartons absorbed enough vibration to hold the camera steady but pointed in the direction of travel. This was before image stabilization technology.

The first time it was to show a motorcyclist's view of the highway where he crashed. It came out great, good clear image. Another time it was to establish the visibility of oncoming traffic at a driveway, another success.

Clients wanted more sophistication so we got a helmet

camera, mounted it on my helmet. One case involved a tractor trailer turning across the path of a motorcycle. We hired a flatbed trailer with an adjustable wheelbase so we would have a rig that would have the same maneuverability as the one on the crash. We laid out the evidence on the road at the scene with several cameras, including one on the trailer. The videos were a success in showing that there was plenty of room for the motorcyclist to evade. The helmet cam though made every movement of the rider's head seems erratic.

Some cases are bizarre. In one case a motorcycle collided with a dinosaur. No, it wasn't a T Rex. Dinosaur is trucker slang for the oversize rigs that deliver new cars to the dealer. This one was about 85 feet long. These rigs cannot make a right turn at most intersections. They have to go around the block making 3 lefts. Our driver client got off the freeway and turned left. Then he noticed the addresses were going the wrong way. That necessitated a U-turn., which could require up to 6 lefts. This was before internet maps. First, he had to find a street wide enough for the first left. As luck would have it, he came upon another dealership where other dinosaurs must turn also. He lined up for the turn and waited. He needed over 15 seconds to make the turn. When the traffic light at the next intersection turned red and all the traffic in between was clear he began his turn. When the light changed green the motorcyclist accelerated and managed to hit the taillight of the trailer, with his right leg at 60 mph. In a 45 mph zone. On the wrong side of the road.

I re-enacted the scenario, except for hitting the truck. We bought an identical bike a Yamaha FJ350 set up multiple video cameras and showed it was nearly impossible for the motorcycle to get to the truck in the time between the light changing green and his impact on the rear of the truck. It was barely possible for me to get from the traffic light to the point of impact in the time it took the truck to get there. The truck was in front of the motorcycle for 14 seconds but the rider continued to accelerate. He claimed the truck violated his right of way. It was clear that when the truck initiated his turn the bike was stopped at a red signal. It is preposterous to think a truck weighing over 60,000 pounds can do anything so suddenly that a motorcyclist can't evade.

After the case settled, I discovered that I had not maximized the available acceleration, but I don't think it mattered. That engine power just kept building right up to red line. It might have been wheelie on punch capable, but I never found out.

The other bizarre issue in the case: The plaintiff was uninsured which reduces his ability to make a claim, but claimed he was on the clock, therefore insured by his employer. Actually, he was coming back from lunch. He claimed that he had taken a video home to edit because he had better equipment at home. The video was never introduced.

I investigated another case involving a young man, experienced motorcyclist who decided to upgrade to a bigger bike so he could ride longer distances. They sold him a Kawasaki Ninja 1000. It's a respected bike with insane performance plus durability. Many Police bikes are based on its cousin the KZ1000. The dealer offered him instruction. That consisted of one lap around the parking lot a little more than my Honda Dream experience; he actually got to put the tires on the ground. He was having trouble and said the bike was running poorly. They told him he just needed practice and left; it was closing time. He fiddled with something and engaged the clutch. Next thing he knew he was accelerating beyond his control out of the parking lot across the highway where he got T-boned by a pickup. He became a paraplegic as a result. He sued Kawasaki and the dealer. They deposed him for a week. Deposition, there is a word not in common use. A deposition is a somewhat formal proceeding where lawyers attempt to learn as much as they can, and also intimidate the witness for the future. Deposed can mean exposed as a liar (legal system), or removed from power (politics).

The frustration led him eventually to suicide. Kawasaki and the dealer got off. They deposed me for a day with questions like have you ever studied a vaguely worded but specific sounding course title, probably 50 times. I would reply not by that name and we would move on, Typically, someone gave the junior attorney a list of questions, with no backup information. That happens a lot. We never got to finish the investigation, but I suspect he was trying to ride with the choke on or the fuel tap off. Once he corrected the error, that the salesman should have caught, the bike had full power and accelerated faster than he had ever expected. Attorneys often asked me to give them a list of questions to ask me. My response was a list points to which I can competently answer. They rarely used it, but instead might ask me things that we had never discussed.

In addition to riding long distances to inspections, Cindy and I would ride the motorcycle whenever not limited by capacity or weather, as I did with my inspection trips, we would take the long way home. We never had sex on a moving motorcycle, but that does not eliminate foreplay. Motorcycles are more stable at speed than most non riders probably expect. The rider's left hand is free to go anywhere it can reach. The left hands duties are mostly easy to delegate: Steering, right hand alone, sometimes no hands. Clutch, with a little coordination most motorcycle transmissions are easily shifted without using the clutch, except starting off. That leaves turn signal, high beam and horn which only take second now and then. Late on hot summer nights in the desert a lot of clothing came off, but we never encountered anyone who could be offended.

Cindy's sister invited us to spend a week in Kauai. We decided it would be fun to rent a motorcycle, and Harleys were what is usually available so that was the choice. I was surprised when they did not give me a key. They said "It's a small island". Harley ignition does not require a key and they did not have a fork lock, just lugs for a padlock. We were able to explore most of Kauai in that week. There is only one highway and it does not even go all the way around *Kauai*. End to end is about 100 miles. One evening we decided to go to *Ke'e* beach at the north end of highway 560. It is a quaint 20-minute ride from Princeville over several broken and jury-rigged bridges. One, one lane bridge fell down at one end, so they just put rock fill on top of the sloped bridge and paved it. When we got to the beach, I parked the motorcycle. We got off and realized once we were a few steps from the bike that could not see at all. We turned back to the bike and I was only able to find it by holding up my hand to feel the radiant heat from the engine. We got back on of course and just as I started the engine rain came down like Niagara Falls. Helmets were not required in Hawaii, nor were they even offered. It took an hour and a half to get back to the condo at about 10 mph with my left hand serving as a visor so I could see. Cindy had to bury her face in my back. Sometimes on Kauai it can rain like that for a week, but it stopped about ten minutes after we got back.

The extra maneuverability of a bike made some extra exploration possible. We thought about someday moving there so we stopped and talked to a lot of people most of who seemed to be somebody's gardener or maid. They would tell us of the famous people who owned houses there, but were never home. It did not seem like a good social situation for us. The only full- time neighbors would be the maids and gardeners. I doubt if the week a year Hollywood types would be interested in us. Prices were mind blowing, like a million for a small lot in Hanalei where all the houses were all built 12 feet above the ground for tsunami protection.

We stopped to look at a quaint cemetery and Cindy tried to get off with a water bottle in one hand and her camera in the other, lost her balance and came down hard on her elbow. When you fall down in Hawaii you usually land on rock, she did. She was brave about it, but the next morning it did not look good. We found a Doctor's office and crashed it early without an appointment. The doctor was very accommodating and we even visited for a while, talked about his back pain surgery and my back pain recovery without surgery. He even called Cindy's dad, also a doctor, on the phone. One interesting instruction was to stay out of the river or fresh water pools to avoid infection. He was not concerned about ocean water though.

On a different trip we rented a Harley on the Big Island. We put a lot of miles on it including going all the way around the perimeter about 250 miles with no mishaps. We looked at Waipio Valley. The steepest hill in the state; it averages 25% but in places is probably 40% and often wet. It is also so narrow that downhill traffic must stop at certain points to permit uphill to pass. It was tempting to go down, but the signs FOUR WHEEL DRIVE REQUIRED were pretty intimidating. Even though motorcycles often can handle conditions that two-wheel drive can't we decided to err on the side of safety. Years later having driven that road it's clear we made the right decision. The upside-down wrecks in the woods are very convincing. It was on that trip that we bought our 47 acres. Now the additional sign says NO ALL-WHEEL DRIVE.

I personally put over 100,000 miles on the K bike and only sold it because a car hit it and insurance called it a total although it was still very rideable. I got a call from the man who bought it at auction, just to get the luggage to put on another bike he had. After test riding the K100 he decided to keep it to ride instead.

The bike was relatively trouble free, but there were some maintenance items that should have been simple yet were beyond me. Some light bulbs could only be replaced with great difficulty or extensive disassembly. The most mysterious was a problem with the fuel system. Sometimes the bike would stall, or refuse to start. It had an electric fuel pump in the gas tank. That does not sound safe, but it's pretty standard, there's no oxygen at the bottom of a fuel tank. When it refused to start, I could not hear the fuel pump that normally makes a faint whirring sound so I suspected the pump as the cause. Back when I was in the army, I had a 1956 deuce and a half that is M211 two-and-a-half-ton truck assigned to me that had the same problem. The fuel pump in the saddle tank was supposed to click. If the truck stalled, I would get out and jump on the tank until the clicking started up. I could not very well jump on the bike, but I could get off and shake it. That always worked, but who knows for how long. I decided it would be a good idea to replace the pump.

I looked up the procedure and it was not too frightening so I decided to do it myself. I bought a new pump and drained the gas tank. The filler cap fitting was removable to permit easy access. I wanted to make sure I got every molecule of gasoline out of the tank so that if I made a spark nothing would happen. I blew air into the tank with a shop vac for many minutes after the smell was gone. When I went to pry the old pump out, I found that it was loose, banging around in the tank, probably making sparks submerged in gasoline, but no air. I took it out and tested it. Decided to save $250, snapped it back in and took the new pump still sealed in the package back to the dealer. I never had the problem again.

Sometimes we do things we know we should not. Once on my way to Pasadena I ran over some sharp debris in the freeway. This is rare because traffic usually sweeps it away. I soon realized I had a flat. I had a tire inflator and aired up to get to a service station where I bought a tire plug kit. There were two punctures though and although I got one to hold the other failed repeatedly. I got my assignment done then plugged and reinflated my way home. I tried to get the tire repaired or replaced at Chaparral® in Riverside. They may be the biggest motorcycle accessory dealer in the world. I used to patronize them for tires and helmets. Well, by then it seemed to have grown bigger than a Costco®, they were so big that someone with a problem was a nuisance. They do not plug tires. If I bought a new tire from department T, then I could make an appointment with department R and could have a tire installed in a couple of days. No thanks, plug and pump. At home I had some Safety Seal® tire plugs that my friend and off-road Guru Harry gave me. They worked; they always work. I told this story to my friends at *Brattin* about Safety Seal, but their policy was only to remove and repair from the inside. I think the flat causing object was not a nail, but ragged machining chip. The plug could not make an intimate contact it needed to seal. The plug kit said to limit speed to 50 mph and just go far enough to get a proper repair, but I wound up riding 100 miles at up to 80 mph. Maybe that was why the ordinary plugs leaked. My experience with Safety Seal plugs has been excellent. I did have a sidewall cut on my truck that Safety Seal would not completely seal, but they tell you not to even try that. That held for a month, but I could not get the slow leak to quit.

One other time I discovered a cut in a relatively new front tire. It was still holding air, but the number of cut cords worried me and I replaced it even though it might have been good for 12000 miles.

1150RT

I treated myself to a brand-new BMW R1150RT, *oilhead* boxer, the same bike the CHP uses. The officers praise this bike to no end. One officer said he would pay for it with his own money if necessary, to keep it. It was without a doubt the most comfortable bike I have ever owned. The first bike I ever had that did not need an air horn because the factory horn was just as loud.

It had a great factory sound system and an intercom cell phone hookup. They charge for a two-hour installation even though the factory has already installed the wiring harness and it takes the dealer about 2 minutes to connect it. I even gave in and spent $90 for a Throttle Meister ® device that lets you lock the throttle and give your right hand a rest. That was worth it. It came with an all-inclusive 500-mile special warranty. I used that up the first day! I used up the factory 24,000-mile warranty the first year, with no claims.

Back when the R60 was designed cornering speeds were limited by tire traction, but as tires improved, lean angle had to increase to keep up. The first boxer twins had the camshaft above the crankshaft because that was the obvious arrangement. For one thing they depended on the crankshaft splashing in the oil to distribute oil to the rest of the engine like a Model T. The R100 generation they wanted to mount the cylinders higher for improved, more competitive cornering clearance so they put the camshaft below and added an oil pump. The oilhead went further and added an overhead camshaft in each head which raised the center of gravity. Not an issue at speed, but can make handling at very low speed a little tricky.

I was in the men's room of the Santa Monica Courthouse soaked to the skin. I had to be ready to go on the stand in 15. The weather had been typical Southern California, clear and bright with a few clouds. After I stopped for lunch not far away, I got back on the freeway. The moment I was irretrievably committed the monsoon broke out and I could barely see my way. I missed the exit and the next one was twice as far plus the return trip. Now my white shirt was half dark and half-light like a deformed penguin but at least my other clothes were dry from being in my trunk or dark and did not show it. There was no way to get the shirt dry in time, so instead in desperation I took it off and wet it all over. Apparently, no one noticed!

I did a site inspection on Highway 58 inland from St Luis Obispo. I was about to give up in frustration when I hit an irregularity in the pavement that could have been a problem for novice riders, that saved the day for my client and insured I would get paid. No matter how big a retainer one gets from a plaintiff lawyer there is always the risk of expenses exceeding the retainer and being unable to obtain compensation. I turned to go home and the rain came down almost as hard in as Santa Monica, all the way home, 5 hours. I was equipped for that, but I kept saying to myself "I'm too old for this shit." My only real problem though was keeping my cell phone mic dry.

I made the mistake of swearing this was a bike I would never drop. Then I dropped it, more than once. The engine was more modern than the R100. It had overhead camshafts. To do that they had to make the cylinders even higher. That made which made the center of gravity higher and the bike more likely to upset at low speed, embarrassing to say the least. High engine center of gravity was one reason. The other was my heavy equipment box on the seat.

Not only did it upset at walking speed more easily than

the R100 but the valve mechanism covers were fragile. Previous *Beemers* had thick heavy covers that could take a licking. When a boxer twin falls over, that's what it lands on. I had to buy three for this bike. Just knocking it over could break one. The covers were about $100 but I could buy a plastic guard for $80 and should have. We went to the Claremont movie theater frequently. I could park in the huge lot in front search for a space and walk a block to the door, or the small lot behind about 100 feet to the door. I did that for years. One-night vandals tipped the bike over, the hard way to the left, over the side-stand. I found it in a puddle of oil. The valve cover of course was smashed. I made it home leaking a little oil. Mall security gave me permission to park it in the bicycle rack by the front door from then on.

This bike was not very maintenance friendly either. Simple jobs like changing some light bulbs required removing 18 screws. They were the same size but different lengths and not interchangeable. What annoyed me most was that the battery was equally inaccessible. You could not use jumper cables if the battery was dead. By the way a car battery can jump a motorcycle battery safely as long as they are both twelve volts, and the user follows safe procedure. Some people say you can't because of the physical size difference. That does not matter. They are both twelve-volt (Actually about up to 14.3 at full charge). Twelve volts is twelve volts no matter how big the twelve-volt battery looks. You can jump a 6volt car with a 12volt battery. At B&W they had a battery the size of a desk in a dedicated Cushman Truckster® three-wheeler to start the in-plant locomotive, or any recalcitrant car in the winter. This seems to be the trend in everything automotive, as things become more reliable, they have fewer things to service and less engineering effort into serviceability. Some believe that this is an effort to give the dealers more service-related income.

All in all, I enjoyed this bike immensely; the national speed limit was gone and speeds on California interstates went even higher. I remember riding this bike 100mph on busy I5 in Orange County and being passed! People would ask me how fast it could go and my answer was "I don't know but at 110 it's not even breathing hard." I got a few speeding tickets. Once as I came out of the Laguna Mountain pass on I8 at about 110 I saw a CHP car on the Ocotillo on- ramp. I was able to slow down quickly and by the times he got behind me I was going 65. The officer was very polite and patient. Not all are, some are downright rude. She advised me that the court system was backed up and I should call the court to schedule a hearing date rather than appear as instructed on the citation. It took many iterations over several months to schedule a date. As with most tickets one hopes the officer will not appear and the charge will be dismissed. I had time to enjoy wandering the 100-year-old courthouse, built before California considered real courthouses a waste of money. I settled in at the appointed place and time. The officer was there. The judge asked the officer if she had observed me speeding and she answered honestly, "No". The judge then asked if the pilot was present, he was not. The pilot of course is the CHP officer who clocked me from 8000 feet above. Without him, and the other officer's honesty the judge had no choice but to dismiss. That did not stop the judge from lecturing me.

Courthouses ought to have an air of permanence and dignity. Most do. Federal courtrooms are the size of a hotel ballroom with lots of fine wood or marble, on the other hand I have testified in courtrooms that were trailers, hotel rooms, converted warehouses and one trial was held in a dead-end hallway.

The inconvenience of a ticket every few years does not deter the majority of drivers from driving the speed they believe is safe and efficient rather than the arbitrary one determined by a politician or bureaucrat who may have never seen the road. Eight Hawaiian Islands are each unique. For a bureaucrat in Honolulu to make decisions for the big island is like having an clerk in Miami Beach make decisions for Colorado or Texas, but that's the way they do it. Hawaii Island is six times as big as Oahu. We have people with 80-mile commutes and a 35 mph speed limit.

About half the traffic tickets in America are dismissed at trial for one reason or another. About half the tickets are for speeding and it is widely believed that the main purpose of speeding tickets is revenue, not safety. I have heard things from reliable people, like a police captain, and a traffic engineer that they get pressured to bring in the revenue. San Diego County was asking for state funding for something unrelated to traffic like a school and the message back from the legislature was you did not send in enough traffic fine money. If even half the people who get traffic tickets went to court, even to plead guilty the system would collapse. I call it a reverse lottery.

Two things about motorcycles are controversial among non-riders. One is no hands riding. Riding with no hands is surprisingly secure but it does increase reaction time. The spinning parts are like gyroscopes. Luke again advised me the bike will take care of you. Most perturbations of the bike will die out naturally before you can even react. There are riders who routinely perform stunts that are amazing. I'm not that bold but letting go so you can stretch makes long rides easier. The RT was particularly stable. It was possible to change a jacket while riding on the freeway.

The other controversy is lane splitting. Non riders almost universally disapprove, but again it does not look nearly as dangerous from the bike as from the car being passed. Riding safely means being in control and responsible for your own situation. Motorcycle officers describe it as moving up on traffic. That is how they ride, so they are in control of the passing interaction. A rider sees freeway traffic as a sheet of obstacles with a few random deviants that happens to be moving along with him. The speed relative to the other vehicles is much more important that their collective speed over the ground. The individual vehicles can be passed one at a time safely and that minimizes interaction with the deviants. There are some riders who do it way to fast, but that's really a separate issue. I once followed a CHP officer about 10 miles splitting lanes on I5. We were passing a lot of cars, but at a speed difference similar to walking past parked cars. A motorcycle in queue with traffic becomes invisible and likely to be hit by someone changing lanes abruptly or caught between two cars braking in response to the car in front but unable to avoid crushing the bike in between. Splitting is permitted in California. Technically not illegal because a California judge once ruled that a motorcycle since it is only one tire wide cannot be in two lanes at the same time which would be illegal according to the California vehicle code. Motorcycles can ride side by side in one lane, but for safety it is recommended that they be staggered to minimize the risk of collision.

Some freeways have a simulated island between the car pool lane and the fast lane. People call it the motorcycle lane and it's was not clear to me clear whether CHP would write a ticket for riding there. I never got one. One reason I bought the RT instead of the more luxurious models was the overall width. I knew I could not resist lane splitting and wanted to make it as safe as practical.

The R1150RT, my favorite ride

The RT was so comfortable I decided to do the Iron Butt Challenge. Ride 1000 miles in under 24 hours. I had ridden San Diego to Santa Cruz 900 miles and San Diego to Fresno 700 miles with additional local driving near Fresno, several times. The Iron Butt association's required evidence gas receipts as evidence and a couple of witnesses. The only extras on my bike were a sheepskin seat cover, every bike should have one, and two extra foot pegs set forward to allow a range of sitting positions. The Iron Butt association recommends taking meal breaks and fuel breaks at separate stops. Usually, I combine them. I followed their advice and rode from San Diego to Sacramento following parallel routes up and back. I left at the crack of dawn, and was home before dark with about 1100 new miles on the clock. I could have done a few hundred more. A five-minute break once an hour really does make the day more comfortable no matter what you are doing in between.

Riding long distances is an interesting radio experience. Most of the time in rural California you can get four strong stations: Country, popular, Spanish, and talk. It only takes a minute to scroll though the selection. In LA though there are so many stations, I think at least 80, that unless you know the frequency of the kind you like, the scrolling is endless. You can find a song you like but it turns out to be a Hmong language station that plays one pop song a day or once a week.

In 2005 we decided to take three month motorhome vacation. We planned to make it a summer trip so we bought a folding boat, and a rack for Cindy's little Honda. We spent a lot of time preparing the motorhome for our comfort.

Let's take a break here. While I was enjoying the RT, Cindy decided to learn to ride. I showed her things like counter-steering as she watched over my shoulder. Push one handlebar with one finger and the bike turns that way. The opposite of what a novice expects. Lots of people have trouble with that concept which is why I had made a video demonstration. She took the Motorcycle Safety Foundation, Safe Rider Course designed by my friend Luke 20 years before. She completed the course with no difficulty. To ensure her safety, we took rides all over San Diego County, sometimes I lead to set an example sometimes I followed and then did a critique. Cindy is a fast learner, but she dropped that bike more times in a month than I do in a decade and she decided not to continue to ride when we moved to Hawaii.

The little Honda seemed secure on the rack behind the motor home, but at the end of day one we found it leaning 45 degrees and apparently ready to fall off. Needless to say, we doubled the attachment to the RV.

SEE PART TWO

Taking the bike along was a two-part decision, a back-up incase the motorhome let us down. A motorhome is like having a car, house and boat all in one, there are that many things that can go wrong. Seldom did a day go by that something didn't need to be fixed or adjusted. I can remember making a suspension repair on a Wyoming Highway. The other reason was to be able to make side trips. I only remember two. One, we were camped at Lake Powel; we used the Honda Rebel to go into town take a tour of the museum and see a movie. An awful movie. After the movie I realized my only glasses were sunglasses. Not good for riding in the dark. We went into Longs and I picked out a pair of clear bifocal reading glasses that would protect my eyes. Cindy did not like the style and switched them with another pair. That would have been alright, but the other pair were not bifocal and I would have been unable to focus past my watch. Fortunately, they let me exchange.

The other time was Zion Canyon. There are lots of highway overlooks impossible to a motorhome or even a car that easily accommodate a bike. After driving through the famous tunnel, we decided to rerun the trip on the bike because the motorhome is so constrained. No one is allowed to park in the tunnel anymore, so the view from the tunnel windows is limited to a quick glance as you go by. The tunnel is rounded it cannot accommodate large vehicles in both directions at the same time. The park service accumulates motorhomes and trucks on the side then changes the tunnel to one way to accommodate a caravan periodically.

When we got back to San Diego the RT's battery was dead and nearly impossible to reach to jump start, 18 screws. I took a chance rolled it down the alley, successfully bump started it and rode it until the battery was charged.

Later we took another extended vacation. This time I left a tender on the battery when we came back the battery was OK but the ABS module had gone bad $2,500. I was going to sell it rather than take it to Hawaii, so I sold it then. There is no BMW motorcycle service in Hawaii.

My last big court case was against Harley. My national reputation brought me a product liability case against them. I was skeptical of the defect, and its link to the fatal crash, but the client was willing to pay all cost up front to have me fly to the crash location and examine the vehicle and the scene, after which I expected to be telling him to forget it. The investigating officer had concluded that the accident could not be reconstructed, and considering his failure to collect any evidence, he was right. I never should have agreed with him though. That made it possible to unreasonably limit my testimony. After examining the scene and the vehicle I became convinced that the case had merit. I asked for two things to be done. Have the scene mapped by a licensed surveyor; give me reprints of the contemporaneous photographs taken at the scene.

West Virginia is different. The only state entirely within Appalachia. My time in West Virginia was an education all its own. We went to a law office in a house so dilapidated that it threatened to fall over at any moment. Nearby there were hundreds of idled cabooses with solar panels on top. Freight trains no longer have a caboose. Norfolk Southern Railway ran through the town, but half the locomotives were BNSF, a western railroad. Guns were everywhere. On the 60-mile commute from his home in Charleston to his office in Williamson the client suddenly handed me his loaded .45 to admire. He kept three loaded pistols within reach of the driver's seat, a pistol within reach of any seating position plus a shotgun and rifle in the back.

During the inspection of the plaintiff's motorcycle someone came by and asked if anyone knew the location of a house with a grey Ford Taurus on the front porch, upside down. A local just asked, "Which one?" as if that was as common as an engine tree. You still see those in West Virginia. To extract a worn-out engine without proper equipment the method is to jack up the car under a tree. Chain the engine to a husky limb, then lower the car. It's seems customary to leave it there, for parts, I guess.

Back at the clients house he showed me his new anti-sniper rifle, then took me to a road house for sea-food, in Appalachia. It was good and I enjoyed some dishes I would not have ordered, like Monkfish. He was going to have me stay at his house, but the dogs made that impossible.

The client spent lavishly on everything, my wife and I were wined and dined in San Diego he took us to an expensive restaurant and after dinner ordered all the desserts. The two things I had asked for to support my opinion he never obtained.

The only thing useful was a detailed summary of the manufacturer's warranty repair records. The search showed that the model had a history of engine unstart due to an overheated fuse. There were hundreds of photographs taken a year after the crash, after the scene was modified. We were never empowered to do any testing or disassembly on our own. The defense spent lavishly on many things including test crashes, one of which almost exactly duplicated my theory as to how the crash happened.

The survey of the scene was never performed. I only got to see the timely photographs twice, at my original inspection and at the trial. I was deposed three times. At the first deposition I disposed of all six hypotheses under which the case had been filed and instead proposed a simpler more viable one based on the defect for which there was statistical evidence. At the second and third depositions, to my shame, I was coerced to testify about things that I did not have first-hand knowledge about.

The plaintiff did not have motorcycle license, but the crash scene highway was a link in the Hatfield-McCoy Trail that was really for dirt bikes, and bicycles and had an exception for the trail to the state license law. My client used that exception to argue that the lack of a motorcycle license was therefore irrelevant at the location of the crash.

The lawyer spent lavishly to bring in witnesses from out of town and to keep me in town for the entire trial. (Well, he still owes for much of that.) At trial the plaintiff lawyer spent most of his effort coaching percipient testimony more favorable to his case. My own testimony was abbreviated by both lawyers' eagerness to conclude it on a Friday evening. I made it clear that the defect was latent, transient and statistical. There could be no tangible defect, no smoking gun. I compared it to a snake in the woodpile, usually it won't bite, but it could.

My client refused to take my advice about a number of things:

1. He insisted that I continue to dispute the testimony of an expert who was obviously very well informed, unimpeachable, and not important.
2. He declined however to have me rebut an expert whose entire opinion was based on circular logic. "Assuming the decedents perception, reaction time was twice the normal we come to the conclusion that he was inattentive because his perception time was so long."
3. He declined to make an effort to admit into evidence the critical photograph that showed the huge boulder hidden in the weeds in the right of way. My entire opinion, which I never got to express, was based on the very likely scenario that the rider experienced an unstart and rolled to the shoulder where the motorcycle crashed into and was upset by that boulder.
4. He insisted on crediting me with work obviously done by others.

A final plaintiffs witness was very favorable and well received, though not particularly important. My client became obsessed with his "momentum" and went directly to closing. Although he talked about staying up all night preparing, as of midnight he had not started.

The defense closing argument consisted of a lot of lies about me, made credible by the things I never got to do, and a comment that the plaintiff never produced a tangible defect, as if a defect had to be something you could throw for the dog to fetch. The plaintiff closing was an exaggeration and purely emotional appeal. The snake in the woodpile analogy became a power tool that explodes if you use it.

Until the closing the Harley lawyer was friendly to me, to the point of recalling warmly a previous case that they ultimately lost after I testified against Harley. I had inspected that bike at their factory and witnessed a pointless demonstration by their expert in Phoenix. That case involved a Harley that leaked oil onto the rear tire and loss of control on an industrial street in New Jersey. Their expert brushed a small amount of oil on a new tire then rode a motorcycle around on a skip pad of sunbaked Arizona asphalt that probably could have absorbed gallons of oil before it became slippery.

I was asked, on the cusp of the moment to testify about damages, a subject for which I had no basis, qualification or experience, and I said so as I begged a ride to the airport. Before my plane left, I got a phone call that the jury came back with a defense verdict. Ironically, the lawyer lamented that it was too bad he and I did not get together at the beginning of my career, and proposed that we write a book jointly on how these cases should be pursued. This is my contribution. I don't expect his anytime soon.

KLRs

I was not in Hawaii long before I felt the need of another motor. Sure, a car will always get you there but there is a feeling of freedom on a bike, whether real or imagined that a cage can't match. The same speed seems faster, and parking is never far from the destination. I decided to look for a Kawasaki 650KLR. It had a good reputation for reliability and plenty of power for an island. I thought the off-road capability would be handy. It was not hard to find two. They about were the same price, age and mileage. The one I chose was at a dealership so I felt there was less chance of a hidden effect.

The factory windshield was a little low for my taste, so I added a clear plastic spacer to raise it about 9 inches and that greatly improved weather protection and highway comfort. Wind resistance can be quite tiring. I also added an air horn because the factory horns are only useful to salute friends in the parking lot, I've had ring-tones that get more attention. Motorcycles are invisible. That is one reason police use them. I bought a pair of bicycle baskets at Wal-Mart for $15. A milk box on the luggage carrier completed my customizing. Open top luggage was very convenient and nothing was ever stolen. I did have a glove or two blow out. For some unexplainable reason if I lose or destroy a glove its always the left one. For years I wore a right glove turned inside out on my left hand. It actually went on and off more easily. There are all kinds of expensive motorcycle gloves. For the most part I have found inexpensive truckers gloves more than adequate. I had trouble with that milk box getting loose and one time it fell completely off. A driver told me it fell, so I went back to look for pieces and found the box, hardly damaged with all my gear still inside setting on the sidewalk. Theft is not a big problem in South Kona. You have to be a special kind of stupid to be a criminal on an island. There are not a lot of convenient places to hide and population is small enough that you feel everyone knows everyone. Half the hitchhikers I pick up know Mason my stepson, or my wife. Half the time I had to hitchhike someone I knew came along.

I had to make do without my sound system, but an iPod and earbuds seemed adequate, though prohibited by the know nothings in the legislature. It's OK with them if one has a Blaupunkt at 100dB inside a Mercedes that has dual pane soundproof glass, but never headphones. The same brain trust has made it illegal to use a cell phone while driving. They cannot see that since they passed that law total traffic fatalities each year started going up. Fatality numbers that had stayed the same since 1938 in spite of a hundred times the number of miles being driven. To manage the iPod by feel, I cut off the index finger-tip of my left glove.

I got the bike with extra tires. When the front wore out, I decided to swap it. I have mounted many motorcycle tires myself, but this very narrow tire was so stiff it was beyond me. This confirmed my opinion of an investigation I did many years before. An after-market Simi Valley shop sold tires to a retired LAPD officer. All the customers seemed to be retired LAPD with beards and long gray hair. The bike was in storage for about a year before the owner took it out riding with a friend. He lost control and crashed. The tire had unseated, that is come off the rim and except for being captured on the same axle was disconnected but flopping around. This caused impossible handling. No one could find a defect in the tire or rim. It was also a narrow and very heavily constructed tire. I think it was load range C tire like a tire for a heavy-duty pickup. Even though the bike was in storage for a year no one had checked the tire pressures before riding.

The KLR served me well most of the time, but suffered from occasional engine unstarts. By unstart I mean engine failing to run for no apparent reason. As if the ignition was switched off.

Unstart is a pilot's term to distinguish it from a stall. Stall to a pilot means lack of lift. Not the same as stalling because I overloaded the engine. It always restarted within a few seconds. There came a time when it just would not start and was as dead as if the battery was disconnected. My daughter Ali and son in law Mike, were visiting and I was able to call and have Mike come with my truck. There was also an unusual sewer manhole configuration that I was able use like a loading platform to put the bike into the truck. We took it to the dealer who fixed it and said it was just the start-neutral interlock switch. That frankly did not explain why absolutely nothing electrical would work not even the headlight, nor did it eliminate the random unstart problem.

The KLR has a great reputation for reliability, but has lots of interlocks like the neutral start switch that can disable the bike and strand you if you don't know what to bypass.

KLR is what they call a dual sport bike meaning it's a street-legal dirt bike. I was never really comfortable with it off pavement though. Two reasons: in Hawaii what isn't paved is gravel and gravel traction is unpredictable, that means to be stable you have to go at least 15 mph. At 15 or more on gravel, if you do go down you will get bruised or worse. That is the reason most off roaders are armored, usually with fiberglass or engineered plastic. For off road the KLR had lots of ground clearance, but that meant I could not touch down both feet at the same time. That's OK as long as you are moving, but can be inconvenient when you stop, especially if the stop is unplanned. I fixed that with some special links added to the rear suspension. Interestingly when I was on a big Harley rental years before. I felt reasonably comfortable on an unimproved road. There is a very stable feeling about them, low seat, low center of gravity and wide handlebars contribute.

The KLR let me down two other times, but that was just a dead battery. One time I left the key on and drained it. I tried to bump start it, but laid it down instead. We just loaded it in my neighbor's truck and took it home and put it on a charger. The other time I was at a Rotary meeting at the Royal Kona the engine cranked a bit, but would not start. I rolled it downhill and tried to bump start, but no luck. By this time all my colleagues had left so I was on my own. I figured that since I had ridden it an hour before and not left anything on the problem was just an old battery. I decided to replace it right there.

To take the old battery out I had to bend a bracket because a screw was rusted solid. I saw that it was out of electrolyte so I called the dealer and bought a new battery on the phone. By the time I walked there they had it charged. I hitchhiked back. When you are hitchhiking with motor parts in your hand it does not take long to get a ride. I installed the battery and it started right up. That the old battery had no electrolyte in it was *mea culpa*. The battery was installed inside the frame where the only way to check the battery water, except for one end cell was to disconnect it and take it out. Even checking that cell was hard because the clear case darkens and becomes virtually opaque. This is a growing trend in automotive design. As things become more reliable, they get harder to access for service. At least cars still have the battery where you can see it, although it is sealed so you can't check the electrolyte.

One thing Kawasaki pioneered is called bucket shim valve adjustment. Instead of opening a cover and adjusting the valve lash with a pair of wrenches and a feeler gauge it became a shop job. The old way could be done at home or on the side of the road if needed. To do the bucket shim job required taking off the gas tank, removing the cam cover, and measuring the clearance with feeler gauges. So far that's not a big deal except for having to remove the gas tank. Now however one has to record the clearance for each individual valve. There could be as many as 16. Remove the timing chains, remove the camshaft(s) be careful to maintain the right timing. Insert or remove shims from each bucket aka valve lifter to get the correct clearance. If you need a shim, you have to buy a set of various thicknesses even if you only need one. Put it all back together and recheck the clearances. If one isn't right, do it over. Fortunately, a clever mechanic invented a special tool to compress the valve springs. That way you can change the shims without removing the camshaft. The tool is expensive. Names persist: The valve lifter pushes the valve down to open, but it's called a lifter because the old prewar flathead engines had the valve in the cylinder block, the cam pushed it up to open like a bathroom wash basin drain.

South Kona seems to have more bulldozers than lawnmowers. It seems like every block someone has one, or a backhoe, or Bobcat®. Sometimes you see what looks like just a pile of weeds and underneath is an old rusty D8®. You think of it as abandoned junk, then one day it's working a mile away. Lawnmowers are not much use here because most of the land is uneven lava rock. Most of the grass cutting is done with a string trimmer, or modified hedge trimmer. Large areas are mowed with tractor mounted mowers.

I heard there was a Caterpillar D11® here. The biggest tractor made. There is one Komatsu® that depending on how you measure might be slightly larger, but the D11 is king. You will probably never see one. I made two attempts to see it, but the rough rock road intimidated me on the KLR so I took my truck. The series starts with D4 and the tractors are hard to tell from the next larger or smaller, until you get to the D11. D9 is the largest that can be transported on the highway assembled. In California I never saw a D10 or D11. D11 is distinct it is so big it looks like a yellow tugboat on land. More recently I saw 3 D11s on one project. They are actually intended for strip mines.

Anyhow, that rough road convinced me to lower the seat which is most easily accomplished with some special links installed into the rear suspension.

Where I live, we have a collector road that connects the local streets to the state highway. It is very steep, greater than 25% in places. If a motorcycle stops going up that slope, the front brake cannot hold it. The tire just slips. The first time I had this problem a well-meaning friend tried to control it by throwing a 4 by 4 under the front tire, a fraction of a second too late and the bike was totally out of control. It went down and bent my $15 baskets. I tried to learn from that, to always stop on one of the nearly level cross streets.

Unfortunately. I let the oil get too low once and the engine made some strange noises. I drained the oil, hardly any came out and refilled it. It started and died then would not start again. A teardown inspection was minimum $300. My experience with garages was once it's apart they are not likely to say" Gee it looks great." and just put it back together. That would probably be another $300 plus a: while were in there, we should… I decided to write it off, but I still have what's left of it. That I kept for parts.

The remains of my first KLR

Another KLR

SINCE the KLR had been pretty good I decided to find another. It was easier than I expected. I found one that was one year newer with less miles and saddlebags too. The price was really too high, $3,700, but it was exactly what I wanted so I went ahead and bought it on the spot. I knew I had lots of replacement parts including two tires and a chain. I put my special extended windshield on it, my special suspension lowering links and my milk box on the luggage carrier. Weathertight lockable bags were a step up.

I had a flat with this bike in Kailua (aka Kona town) and I knew I could not demount the tire. I figured out that I could take the wheel off and hike about a half mile to the Harley dealer. First problem, Kawasaki did not include in the tool set a wrench big enough to remove the rear axle nut. Fortunately, I was one block from Lowes. I hiked up and bought a cheap set of adjustable wrenches, 4 for the price of 1 ½. Took the wheel off and walked and hitched to Kona HD. In luck they had one tube left in the correct size. The tech that mounted the tire boasted about how he had never pinched a tube. They gave me a ride back to the bike and when I got there the tire was flat. He had pinched the tube. The only one they had. They were gracious and sent a trailer to pick up the bike, took it to the shop and I don't remember whether they found another tube or patched this one. Perhaps I should mention that everyone I have ever dealt with at a Harley dealer has been friendly and courteous, even if I was just doing research for a client who was suing Harley. Even the ones dressed like Hells Angels.

A neighbor asked to have a convex mirror installed across from her driveway that was on a blind curve with a steep slope.

I stopped to look over the situation. The bike slipped downhill, fell over and slid. A passing neighbor helped me get it upright, but it slipped again and this time the handlebar end came down on my left foot. It hurt like a bullet. I estimated the energy, and it was in the range of a pistol bullet. Fortunately, the large area, inch and a quarter diameter, prevented penetration, but it still hurts. I eventually got hold of a bicycle brake lever with cable and made it possible to apply the rear brake with my left hand.

One drawback to the second KLR was that the luggage keys were bright red. I scheduled a speaker for Rotary who did not have a computer and asked me to bring mine. I parked my bike where I usually did behind *Teshima's* where we meet. As I walked up the stairs, I noticed that I had left my keys in the bike ignition but I thought the location was safe. Not the first time I forgot and left the key. The speaker never showed up. When I went to leave my bike was gone. There were video cameras and even a witness but all we got was an average size guy wearing a black hoodie in August. I filed a Police report not that that would do any good. The bike is probably still being used on a farm in Kau or even on the sort of private road system in Hawaiian Ocean View Estates (HOVE) the largest subdivision anywhere with 11,500 one acre lots. Sort of the wild west.

I circulated posters of the stolen bike, but never heard anything. If I ever see it, I can recognize it by some of the details I changed, like a tiny hole in the brake pedal. If that should happen, which is extremely unlikely, I know how to disable it until the cops get there.

HOVE is a funny place. There are people living in truck bodies at the higher elevations and 5-acre estates with stone walls around them a big house, guest houses, 8 car garage, swimming pool etc. closer to the highway; places that would sell for a million or more most places; several million, west of I 5, and everything in between.

I hear HOVE has serious burglary problems. People have had solar water heaters stolen off the roof while they were at work.

Major appliances can disappear if unattended. On the other hand, they have a strong enough sense of community to start their own fire department and have a civic center with popular events. We bought a lot there on spec, but the prices have not gone up in ten years. It is probably the cheapest land in Hawaii with a paved road.

ANOTHER HONDA,
A CTX 700

I needed another bike, well wanted; nobody really needs one unless they have no transportation at all. The need is visceral, not practical. My needs had changed. The plan to go off the grid and live on our 46 acres had been pretty much trashed by *Bushonamics*. It was time to reconsider the specifications.

The KLR, even with the added windshield had inadequate weather protection, and I did not need the off-road ability. In fact, I was never comfortable with it. I needed something with longer legs so I could go to Hilo if need be. I did not see the need to move up to a big tourer like the BMW, a Gold Wing or Harley. I visited the dealers in Kona and found mostly more dual-sport or crotch rockets. There were a few sportsters and a BMW K75, but with no local parts or service it was not attractive to me. A scooter would have better weather protection, but did not fit my self-image. I don't trust the small wheels either. After riding Cindy's little Honda Rebel, I knew I would not be happy with a 250 either. There are some times when the thing that saves you is lots of acceleration power. We teach one another, "When in doubt, screw it on'" that is accelerate away from the danger. It usually works unless the danger is right in front.

An on-line search revealed one mid-size (700ccs) bike with an optional tall windshield and luggage. It also offered anti-lock brakes (ABS), an expensive high maintenance option. Remember, $2,500 to fix the RT. It was also a last year model offered at a substantial discount. I made a low-ball offer if they included the tall windshield and bags. It was accepted. I passed on the ABS and $400 trunk. A $26 tool box worked just as well. The windshield works well and they let me keep the take-off shield, in case. The bags were disappointingly small though, they will not hold a helmet. To me that is a design defect, but on the other hand helmet theft is rare in helmet-optional Hawaii.

My experience with years of *Beemers* was that I could make the front tire howl indicating incipient lockup without locking it up. I did not see the need for $1,500 ABS, which also would have meant a non-leftover therefore even more expensive bike. One day I decided to go 20 miles to Captain Cook Village to buy some little thing instead of waiting until I was going anyway. The driver in front of me was a little unpredictable in that she would speed up or slow for no apparent reason. I held back and did not give her much thought. My mind drifted to something else, and is typical post trauma I cannot remember what. What I do remember is looking ahead and seeing a minivan stopped, about 30 feet in front of me. I grabbed the front brake and locked it up. This caused the bike to upset and slam me into the ground; instantly. I slid to a stop on my left side and just barely impacted the car. My windshield was scratched. My left side had a lot of bleeding road rash. There was a dent on the car, way too high to be related, but an otherwise helpful witness was sure to point it out to the other driver.

I accepted the blame, after all I had rear ended a stopped vehicle. I gave her my card and did not even bother to get her data. I did not want to wait for police to come and create a report. I just wanted to go home and stop the bleeding. I taped my left shoe back together and rode the bike home. It seemed to me that the damage was minor, except that the instrument cluster was smashed. I got the bleeding controlled and bandaged over before Cindy got home to get upset about it.

Two things had to be done. A police report because there was an injury, mine, probably more than $500 property damage and the other driver might report it first. It must have been a slow day for South Kona PD because they sent two officers to my house to follow up. One of the officers I know and would not trust him to do a book report. Fortunately, the rookie took my statement. I called my insurance company about the bike damage. They offered to send a tow- truck to pick up the bike and although I could have ridden it to the shop, I put it on the truck so I would not have to get a ride home.

It took about two weeks to get an appraisal on the bike because the appraiser had to come from Honolulu, that's on a different island for those unfamiliar with Hawaiian geography. The appraiser told me that the bike was totaled. I think she thought that was good news, but considering how hard it was to find that bike at that price I was not happy. Her second offer was somewhat less, but I could keep and repair the bike. I chose that option.

The appraiser and the dealer service adviser came up with similar estimates but were inconsistent in what needed to be replaced. The adviser was somewhat sarcastic suggesting I go along with his estimate, take it home and fix it myself, or take it to an independent shop. I decided to let the dealer fix it based on their estimate. It took months to get the parts. I took the old parts home. I examined them carefully and found that for the most part they had little, no or only cosmetic damage. The adviser had done the estimate as if it was an insurance repair, which it no longer was. I filed a complaint with the management and showed them the undamaged parts that I had been charged for. The acquiesced and agreed to put my old parts back and reduce the bill by over $1,000. Mostly they just adjusted the bill because the parts were not worth the labor to swap them out. That adviser does not work there any-more.

I have been mentally reconstructing that incident and find I made five possible mistakes. I knew the driver in front of me was unpredictable: I should have left extra room. Two: I was not paying enough attention, I don't remember why, but my mind was doing something else. Three: I was not covering the front brake; my right hand was not even on the grip. Four: I grabbed the front brake abruptly and locked the wheel instead of modulating. Five: I may have made some inadvertent steering input. That would explain why the bike capsized instead of a normal stop.

If the bike had stayed upright, it would have stopped short and neither I nor the bike would have had any damage. Lesson learned keep the road in front within my peripheral view and consciousness at all times. If in doubt allow extra following distance. Cover the front brake.

Thrice I rode it to Hilo, 96 miles each way. First time the biggest challenge was finding parking in the shade. There is insufficient parking at the County Building. I took rural Highway 11 eastbound and the infamous saddle road home. Saddle road now State Highway 200 is like a Texas or Montana Highway, 60 feet wide with curves you could navigate at 120 mph. You could land a jumbo jet on it. Unlike Texas or Montana where the speed limit would be 75 it's 55, except where it's 45. I tried to keep it under 60, but the dump trucks passed me like I was tied to a post. A local senator tried to get the limit raised to a more reasonable 65, but the best she could get out of our urban Honolulu based department of transportation was 60, except where it's still 45.

The second time I rode to Hilo I got caught in the rain. I stopped and put on my raingear. In Hawaii rain has an unusual property it's tremendously wet in terms of water. I was wearing Florsheim boots. When I got there, I noticed I was walking funny. The heel washers had dissolved because the material they were made out of was like paper. $200 boots and they used paper! Florsheim honored the warrant though after almost 15 years. I used the certificate to buy some loafers than paid a local shop to replace the washers. It looks like he used the same paper like material, so I know not to get them so wet.

The third time the meeting was cancelled and I did not get the message in time. After that I bought a Bluetooth radio adapter so I know who's calling. I can also listen to music without the ear-buds, although the quality is poor, cheap Chinese junk with inscrutable instructions written by some kid who learned English at a Chinese high school, but that's what I could get.

155

I was generally very pleased with this bike. I even once found myself thinking it was the best ever, but that's only within the Hawaii limitation. It would not do for an iron butt, at least not at my age. One detail I really could do without, which may explain my distraction, is the feet forward riding position. It enables a lower seat, like a Harley, that makes low speed riding feel safer, but it reduces the handling ability and in particular the ability to stand up on the foot- pegs to get a better look. Observed trials type bikes barely have a seat; the riders stand on the pegs most of the time. I have spent a lot of mental energy figuring out how to add pegs I could stand on, but unsuccessfully so far. I did add some heel rests that let me have multiple riding positions.

CAREER TALES

BEING a rider and an engineer put me in a position to be considered an expert. When I hooked up with John Fiske Brown, he taught me traffic accident reconstruction. He quickly decided to transfer the motorcycle cases to me. Soon we wrote a chapter "Motorcycle Accident Reconstruction,[2]" for Automotive Engineering and Litigation. Then a book Forensic Engineering Reconstruction of Accidents together and ultimately along with many lesser publications I wrote Motorcycle Accident Reconstruction[*] – Understanding Motorcycles, which was Lawyers and Judges Publishing's fastest selling title. It grew with subsequent additions to over 600 pages.

In some circles I was considered the leading expert in the subject, because there was only one book and I wrote it. The books led to assignments in at least 21 States that I can recall, 2 Canadian Provinces, 3 Mexican states and a consultation in Germany. Many of the cases resulted in inspection trips as well as depositions and court appearances. Lest you think this sort of travel is glamourous it's not. It often involves an over-night or late-night trip arriving hungry after the last nearby restaurant has closed. Once I arrived to a hotel room near Milwaukee in January, their policy was to turn off the room heat until a guest checked in. It was 8 PM. The only restaurant available was MacDonald's halfway back to the airport. Normally I don't do *MacDoodoo*, but that was the only option. I left the hot shower running to warm up the room while I went back to get food. When I returned nearly an hour later, I could at least take a shower, but the rest of the room was still uncomfortably cold. I wondered how much they saved turning off the heat versus my hour shower.

A trial appearance often involved waiting in the courthouse hallway, or outside the courthouse in the hot sun for hours, or days. I remember sitting on an upturned 5-gallon water bottle in the foyer part of the time. Courts usually keep witnesses outside so their testimony will not be influenced by or especially harmonized with others. In the case of experts this makes no sense, because expert testimony is supposed to be based on the best available information. My testimony often had to be adjusted based on my client telling me, more or less, what witnesses had said, but judges will be judges. One trial judge ruled that my testimony could not change from my deposition testimony six months ago even though there had been much new evidence disclosed. In a few cases I was permitted to sit in on the trial. Perry Mason it's not, nor is it The Verdict. It's more like algebra, where half the time you can't even figure out what's going on. That is because the lawyers try hard to not let the other side tell a cogent story. It can be like watching a TV series out of order with half the episodes missing. Defense in particular works hard to maintain confusion because if the jury cannot conclude beyond a reasonable doubt they are bound to rule for the defense.

Plaintiffs or prosecutors come to court with a tight narrative. They have a point to prove and they have to convince a jury that their story is the certifiable truth. It could not be any other way. In a civil case the plaintiff is usually working on a shoestring, and the defense has almost unlimited funding. In one trial the defense had the courtroom wired to the internet so their legal team of 4 could be in constant contact with the main offices in Washington and Japan. They managed a special dispensation for an out of state specialist lawyer to conduct the defense. There were 350 marked exhibits. The plaintiff had one lawyer and me.

Plaintiff case was simple. He admitted that he fell asleep at the wheel and ran off the road. The fact on trial however was that had the pickup door had flown open during a rollover incident allowing him to be ejected. Had the door stayed closed he would have remained inside and probably not severely injured. That manufacturer had door mechanisms that can open if impacted from the inside. If you know where on the interior trim to kick them, they will fly open.

Defense constantly speculated, in spite of evidence to the contrary, that plaintiff was drunk, and therefore not entitled to compensation no matter what. The judge told them not to do that, but they did it I was told 43 times.

I have great sympathy for jurors. A trial is not like Hollywood's version. Half the time the jurors sit quietly bored while the lawyers and judge whisper to one another at side bar, or withdraw to the judge's chambers. Sometimes after listening to hours of tedious testimony, they are told to disregard it, un-ring the bell. There may be a jury room with the amenities of a bus station waiting room. Cheap metal furniture and if they are lucky a coffee pot or microwave.

Trials I have sat through represent great differences from state to state. California courts seem to keep banker's hours with late start, long lunch and prompt closing. Maybe early closing if the next item on the agenda might not be done until after 4:30. I have even been asked to talk about my qualifications at length so that there would be no testimony for the other side to spend all night analyzing.

In South Carolina, the Circuit Judge was from out of town. It's a very small state, you can drive to the capitol from anywhere in two hours. Testimony started on time. Once a witness was on the stand court remained in session until that witness was finished. The Bailiffs (all black, unarmed) brought in lunch and dinner as necessary. No opportunity for the lawyers to prepare cross exam over-night. Marshalls (all white) maintained order.

Admiral Rickover warned us. If you are going to sin, sin against God, not the bureaucracy. God will forgive you but the bureaucracy won't. One of my cases involved a roofer who fell through a roof. My function was to reconstruct the incident. It was a wooden roof. To assist me I retained a professor from UC Davis.

His expertise was wood products. A purlin had failed under a load that was well within the roof's intended capacity. The professor explained in detail that the beam was out of specification in that there was too much summer wood for select structural. Our client had a satisfactory settlement.

A Civil Engineer who had worked for the lumber mill filed a complaint against me claiming I had encroached on the field of Civil Engineering. Beam design is not proprietary. There can be a beam in a building, a ship, an airplane, car or appliance. His complaint against me was that even though the beam was substandard, it is permissible according to lumber industry standards for up to 10% of the lumber in a batch to be substandard and it's the contractor's responsibility to separate those out! Can you imagine if medicine or food had a provision like that?

We went to court; I accepted my slap on the wrist. The complaint was stayed, but the Board of Registration for Professional Engineers and Land Surveyors (BORPELS) was not satisfied. They published the complaint, but not the resolution. Concurrently I was elected President of the local chapter of the Association of Professional Engineers. There was an inquiry and the State Chapter decided it was irrelevant. BORPELS continued to publish the complaint so that if someone googled my name it came up in the top ten for years and looked like I was still under discipline.

My son has a friend with expertise in Constitutional law. She agreed to Press BORPELS to quit doing it. They heard the argument, agreed, that their action was wrong, then published their half-hearted recession in a way that emphasized the complaint in a way that made me look guilty any time someone googled my name.

California's original licensure law, to protect the public, was titled Civil Engineers. As a result, in California's Civil Engineers have an exalted position that lets them practice any other engineering, qualified or not but prohibits other licensees in any other discipline other than the one for which they are licensed or any practice that a Civil engineer wants to claim. The discipline definitions are vague and overlap. BORPELS is more dedicated to protecting civil engineers from competition that the public from incompetent practice.

Many cases look superficially similar. I warn others, if a case looks just like a previous one, you missed something. The reader might notice that I usually use the term crash, not accident. Almost all crashes have a cause somewhere even though it may be hard to find or be lost in the past. The word accident implies unavoidable, unexpectable or act-of-god.

A number of cases had a similar situation where a vehicle makes a turn across the path of another and the second makes an attempt at an evasive maneuver that is exactly wrong. Biker approaches an intersection. Another vehicle is at the stop sign on his right accelerates across the motorcycles path. The rider instead of going straight and passing behind the other vehicle swerves left hoping perhaps that the other will stop and not cross his path. The bike sideswipes the rear quarter panel of the other vehicle that has actually cleared the straight line the rider could have continued on. I call it leading the target.

A lot of motorcycle cases have to do with visibility, or conspicuity. When they instituted always -on headlight laws motorcycle car crashes went down 40%. We called car making a left turn into the path of a motorcycle the standard motorcycle accident. Drivers do not notice motorcycles, or they see but misjudge the distance, speed and time to impact. Police take advantage of this to catch or entrap violators.

One case involved a Porsche and a police motorcycle. The Porsche approached an intersection normally with a green traffic signal. The Police bike pursuing a speeder entered the intersection diagonally via a wheelchair ramp coming from a parking lot on the corner. They collided just past the intersection. The motorcycle hit the left side of the car. The police officer was injured and cited the Porsche driver for failing to yield to an emergency vehicle (crossing the sidewalk?). The Porsche made skid-marks at an angle to the road leading to the shoulder. This showed that he had indeed attempted to obey the law when he heard, but could not see the police bike.

I liked to think that in most of the crashes, had I been either driver or rider, I could have avoided. One type that scares me that happens too often. A young couple was riding on a country highway near Poway. The wheel lugs on a pickup going the opposite way broke. The 40-pound tire and rim going 40 mph hit the rider also going 40 mph square in the chest. He had no chance.

It is frightening how many cases we got involving tire lug failures. There are a number of scenarios. Lug nuts were loose and unscrewed. Lug nuts were loose and the wobbling wheel bent the studs causing metal fatigue. I actually witnessed one of those while I was doing a site inspection it sounded like a machine gun as all 5 studs broke in one revolution. The tire whizzed by me and the 5 lug nuts with the broken studs in them rattled by my feet. The center hole of the wheel is supposed to fit snugly on the hub and actually carry most of the load. Many after- market wheels have an oversize center hole to fit a variety of vehicles. That way the load is entirely on the lugs. To make it worse, many have slotted holes and depend on a filler piece to align with the studs. Sometimes the filler pieces get lost or badly worn. Sometimes the nuts are what we call blind, or acorn nuts. They look better, because the stud end is concealed. Unfortunately, the stud is too long and instead of securing the wheel to the hub, the stud bottoms in the nut and the wheel is a bit loose, or a lot. Either way the studs will eventually break. Once in a while someone will over-torque the nuts and actually break something. Most tire shops now use a calibrated torque stick between the impact tool and the nut. That is faster and even more accurate than a torque wrench. The really meticulous mechanic will use a torque stick, then double check with a torque wrench. His name is Steve.

Wheel is another word that has different meanings depending on context. Primarily it is the entire rotating assembly on one end of an axle. Including the rotating brake parts, maybe even some non-rotating parts. In the above paragraph I used it to describe the tire and rim assembly detached from the hub and brake. That is the context we use when we call a truck an 18-wheeler, but in reality, it has 8 dual wheels and 2 single wheels. Or it might have 10 super-singles. Or 42 tires in Michigan. If you put dual rear wheels on a 2-wheel drive pickup it's still 2-wheel drive.

There was an on-running childish argument about why trucks had dual wheels. Some said it was needed to carry the weight, but why not just larger single tire. Some said built in spare, but that seemed wasteful. I finally asked my tire expert Oris. He solved the riddle with two words "for safety". Of course, trucks tend to be top heavy and rear end heavy; a rear tire failure would lead to loss of control and possible upset. Dual wheels are extremely unlikely to both fail at the same time. Both arguments were wrong and right.

Motorcycles as I said before are notoriously hard to see. In several cases a car pulled out of a driveway directly into the path of the motorcycle. Naturally the driver says "I never saw him." Usually followed by "Look what he did to my car." There are a lot of reasons for that, but in at least two cases a pole on the drivers left blocked enough vision to hide a motorcycle for more time than the average driver looks. In one case the pole was a 4 x 4 in a center island close enough to the driver's eye to create a blind spot big enough to hide a city bus.

Palomar mountain road in San Diego County is a fun place to test one's motorcycle skills. It is a popular place to crash. Inspecting motorcycle crash scenes, it was not unusual to find parts of multiple other motorcycles that had crashes the same location. Two completely separate cases involved a rider riding along with the same other rider named Deadman. Perhaps competing with him. One too common situation is the rider with tires in his proper lane in the left tire track, where it's normally safest but leaning left across the centerline colliding with an oncoming vehicle that is occupying its entire lane.

A case involved a paraplegic rider riding a sidecar motorcycle on an unpaved county road. The speed limit was posted 25, but rarely obeyed. The rider lost control and went off a steep embankment. He might have been ok but he collided with the very solid wreck of a ready- mix concrete truck that had never been removed. Defense located and retained every sidecar expert that could be found so that plaintiff would not be able to. The government (or corporate) side of every legal action has a budgetary advantage.

Garbage trucks figure into too many motorcycle crashes. Usually, it is because the garbage truck stops unexpectedly, then backs up abruptly. Often the drivers get a full-day's pay when they finish the route. They are motivated to work fast. It is impressive to hear a 40,000- pound vehicle squeal the tires. The motorcycle is not visible in the truck's mirrors because the 8- foot-wide truck body creates a triangular rear blind spot that extends about 400 feet! With no reverse gear the bike cannot back up fast enough and the factory horn is only suitable to annoy pedestrians. The *swamper* who rides on the back is usually pre occupied with the curbside cans and his only communication with the driver is a button mounted high on the truck where he can reach it when standing on the rear platform. Its main purpose is to notify the driver that he needs to stop for a collection. The defense typically argues that the rider should have jumped off and abandoned the bike. The trial judge ruled that my testimony had to be identical to my deposition six months before even though there was new evidence.

Sometimes things do not go well. I was inspecting a motorcycle and needed it to stand up for a photo. To be safe, I went to my van to get a prop stick. As soon as I was out of reach, it fell over. In any case there was no evidence of a defect and I said so. The client refused to pay my bill on the basis that I had spoiled the evidence, even though there was no sign of spoliation. Any superficial damage from the upset would be irrelevant. The big problem was lack of any pertinent evidence. That's what it's like dealing with plaintiff bar. It seems like no matter how much you get in advance from plaintiff bar, you never get all you bill for. They want a triable issue, not facts. Defense is usually more pragmatic and takes their medicine like a big girl if its bitter.

Another worrier was a motorcycle inspection in Houston, Texas. I offered to do the inspection for a fixed price, then discovered the airfare would use it all up. A local travel agent saved the day by booking a flight via Denver. The motorcycle engine seemed frozen and I needed to turn it over that is rotate the crankshaft. I put my wrench on a sturdy looking projection on the clutch disc to turn the engine. Instead, it broke off. I expected a claim but nobody complained.

Good Cop, Bad Cop

CALIFORNIA police policy is that all crashes are caused by a vehicle code violation therefore cops are required to cite a vehicle code violation in their traffic accident reports. If they can't think of anything else, which is about half the time their favorite is 22350, "too fast for conditions". Sometimes it's absurd. A huge timber is knocked off a bridge and falls on a car passing under the bridge, cause "22350, too fast for conditions". The driver should have anticipated falling timber.

I noticed that the crash location was often 528, feet from a landmark, then 1056 feet. I became suspicious, so I watched and sure enough various multiples or submultiples of 1/10 mile, even 264 feet. The officers were using their vehicle odometer that reads out tenths of a mile and converting it to feet. I reported this absurdity to the Chief of the California Highway Patrol (CHP) and to their credit, he told the training supervisor and it stopped. Odometer readings were reported as such, not converted to feet. An odometer reading can easily be off half a tenth, 264 feet, at each end. Useless for accident reconstruction or any investigation.

Even when they use a more accurate device like a Rolatape® two officers can differ by fifty feet or more because their interpretation of the starting point is ambiguous. It gets worse. I went to a crash scene with the injured motorcyclist. The accident report location indicated a mile marker number. When we got there, he said this is not it. I followed him to his recollection of the scene, the difference was 6 miles! The officer apparently mistook the number 7 in his notes for 1. Every physical detail on the report agreed with the client's description, except that the officer thought the blood stain where the injured rides sat waiting for the ambulance was the point of impact. How much blood can drip from a foot in 300 milliseconds?

Our civil justice system is funny. He lost the use of his right foot, and therefore his job so he is entitled to compensation. He found a better job, but he will limp the rest of his life. Oh yeah, I almost forgot, the report sited him for 22350, "too fast for conditions" in reality a station wagon full of rubberneckers crossed centerline and hit him in the middle of his lane.

In an unrelated matter the report referenced the location to Highway 7, but it was near Seventh Avenue, about 5 miles away.

Reports are submitted to a senior officer who then checks them for (hell if I know) consistency with policy. Sometimes they make changes that make the report useless for analysis, and throw in 22350, "too fast for conditions" for good measure.

Two 15-year-olds ran in front of a moped, got knocked down and injured. The moped was going 12 mph. The officer who called the young women children blamed the moped for CVC22350, too fast for conditions. Safe speed zero.

One case involved an off-road dune buggy vehicle on the road. Local officer began his report and then had the vehicle moved to clear the road. A particularly arrogant CHP officer arrived and chased everyone from the scene, including the local officer to whom he refused to listen. The CHP officer then wrote his report on the assumption that he had arrived on an undisturbed scene. He obviously got everything wrong. An alert paralegal noticed that the rest position of the vehicle in the report did not match the photos taken by a witness.

Virginia police reported an absurdly high speed for a motorcycle after it went under a truck. The bike continued a long distance riderless, down an embankment across a highway and impacted with a mountain side. They used the several hundred feet the motorcycle went to calculate its speed ignoring the obvious situation that it was still running and went down an embankment. The rider hit his head on the truck hard enough to crack his helmet so the only relevant fact to calculate speed was the short distance the rider slid. It was not possible to determine how much speed was lost cracking the helmet.

There are lots of other bizarre way officers measure, but these are examples I can explain.

Obviously, the quality of reports can vary for many reasons.

My preference for reports would be like those we got from young rookie rural officers fresh out of accident investigation school. He will have lots of time to try out everything he learned and the report may run 13 pages for a fender bender. On the other hand, an officer on the LA freeways is very busy. Officers in that environment may clean up two fatals before lunch. I once had a report of a pedestrian fatality on an LA freeway. One page, date, report number, mile marker and the decedents name.

A high dollar case involved a farm supply 4x4 one-ton truck. The truck had a wobble problem in the front end, not unusual with what's called a live axle as opposed to independent front suspension like a modern car. The truck went out of control enough to cross the centerline and ran over the police car. Tire tracks on top of the car, emergency lights torn off were irrefutable. The officer had a broken leg from hitting the shotgun that was also broken. The report said on page 2 that the truck did not turn over but on the inner pages it described accompanied by photos that the truck had damage on the roof and one side consistent with a rollover. The lights were knocked off the truck roof too. Somewhere in the editing process rolling over changed to without rolling over. I testified in the criminal case against the driver of the 4x4. The charge was minor, but would make the civil case defense much more difficult. State of California against Jose sounds like Goliath and David. It was obvious Jose could not afford the defense he was getting, so the prosecution wanted to ask who was paying for it. It would be inadmissible to say insurance because that would be an admission that there was insurance coverage. The way I was instructed to word the truthful answer was, "An agent of his employer."

When one end of a rigid axle like that hits a bump, it causes an input to the wheel on the other end, but as with a gyroscope there is a 90-degree lag so the bump becomes a sudden steering input. If there is any looseness in the front end, a wobble can occur which then affects both front wheels. Almost all rigid axle front ends have a hydraulic steering damper (shock absorber) to prevent this wobble. The one on this truck had an incipient defect so the proximate cause was not the driver or owner of the truck but a manufacturing defect. Independent front end does not transmit input like this to the other side, but still might have a steering damper out of an abundance of caution.

The funniest case if any injury crash can be called funny, was a couple on an old Vespa scooter at night in San Diego with no lights, but the passenger held a flashlight inside a red sock as a tail light. The tail light did not matter they T-boned a Volkswagen Jetta.

FINALE

WHEN I started this missive, I did not really expect to ride another half million miles but I was hoping for at least another half a decade. I thought this Honda CTX might be my last bike, but I did not think last would come so soon. I was on my way to a committee meeting at the police station. A green car exited a driveway inconveniently close and that reminded me of my pledge to increased vigilance. Never leave the road ahead outside my peripheral vision. I woke up in the ER! My first thought was "It looks like my motorcycle riding days are over." I remember I think, a white tailgate taller than a pickup tailgate and two brake light, too close. I believe I squeezed the front brake hard and anticipated a crash.

I have never gotten in trouble with the front brake on any other motorcycle, not even when locking it up, at worst a wobble. Rear brake yes, lock the rear and it tries to pass the front, or feels like it. A locked wheel has no directional stability. It will follow the path of least resistance, and that may be to one side. A locked front is already in front, so it has nowhere to go. Luke told me: trust the bike, it will take care of you. Until October 10, 2018, it always had. I laid down a few, but it was sort of like falling off a chair. Except for torn clothing and maybe road rash, walk away. Get the bike back up, get back on and ride away. I read about a rider who laid his down and slid hundreds of feet in full leathers. He was going 140 mph. In my opinion the CTX is defective.

I got: four broken ribs in my back, two also broken in front, two broken toes in my left foot. A brain contusion that could have been fatal, a heart contusion that could have been chronic and road rash scars one of which looked like a gunshot wound. Two months later the foot is what still bothered me. My injuries were consistent with crashing into a wall at 30 mph but I was found just lying in the highway. I probably got what we call a high side, that is launched into the air.

A witness reported stopping to help as traffic whizzed around me. She flagged down someone else to call 911 and that's all I know. I obtained the police report. It had no evidence described, and a point of impact location that in spite of all my experience I could not decipher.

My insurance carrier considered the bike a total even though the damage looked like less than the first time; the expensive instrument cluster was not damaged. Maybe their actuaries want that model off the road, like GM and Corvairs®. It took 5 days in Kona Community Hospital, plus three weeks in bed at home to get to back on my feet, more like six weeks to somewhat normal activity. It was a year before I could consider myself mostly recovered. I still have scars from the road rash. At my age one wonders if residuals are related, or just passing age.

I decided to retain a successful lawyer that I knew, and not shop for one. He had retained me as an expert in the past. His practice is one of the largest in Hawaii. I wanted to sue Honda for a design defect that allowed the front brake to lock too easily, and upset the bike in the process. In a half a million miles I had never had a motorcycle slam me to the ground like that. When the CB350 went down it was like falling off a chair. Every other 'get off' was not from front brake.

I blame myself for one thing. After the first crash with this bike, I should have taken the time to practice emergency braking like I did with the CB fifty years ago. We scheduled an inspection of the bike by the lawyer's expert from Honolulu but once they figured out what that would cost him, he declined to continue. Lack of evidence made it a long shot. Maybe I should have tried harder, but there is a point where one says enough, I don't want to live this for three to five years.

I often got calls from potential plaintiffs asking me if they should sue somebody. If they seemed to have a reasonable case, I might refer them to three potential lawyers, but most of the cases were weak and I would ask questions like how much is your loss and do you really want this to be the main part of your life for 3 to 5 years. Mostly they saw the wisdom of putting it behind them.

One woman worked as a children's birthday party clown. She was not willing to give up. Several lawyers had turned her down. She insisted on having me inspect her car. I did find just the slightest evidence of front-end misalignment. She took my report to the lawyers, but they still declined. She filed the case pro-per, meaning as her own lawyer. She went through the whole process including trial. I explained to the court the slim evidence. The judge was very kind to her, patient. I have noticed that often the judge will give a lot of slack to the weaker party, and she was about the weakest I had ever seen. The judge guided her I thought kindle. Judges are also offended by arrogant lawyers. The defense lawyer was a bulldozer. To my surprise, she won!

PART TWO

TRAVELS WITH BOHBOH

The intrepid Bohboh, he lived 24 years

CALIFORNIA

Twelve weeks, that's a long vacation, hopefully without interruption. I called it practice retirement. We left San Diego back in the Pleistocene age known as September 2005 in a comfy 28foot motor home we call Hulu. Just two grown-ups and a little cat named Bohboh.

Cindy and I were excited from the beginning Bohboh was,

shall I say reticent. He spent most of the daylight hours under the bed, only to come out after dark and tear around like a demon. To his un-catlike credit, he never damaged anything. Boh did spend time on the dash watching the world fly by.

We left our house with a Realtor and a trusted neighbor Emily and we headed north. On the first day we had extra company, our beloved dog Sequoia. We were sad that we couldn't take him with us. He was the best dog ever, but at 16 he is really too old for a new life. Fortunately, he was in love with daughter Megan's Rottweiler, and he retired with them. The dogs both had a love affair with little Paulina so it worked out for everyone, and Daddy Luis was too kind to object. The first leg was uneventful except for the time the refrigerator door came open and dropped two dozen eggs on the floor. One egg survived. You really have to be sure the latch clicks into place. Sequoia licked up the rest.

We arrived close to midnight, parked in front of the house and sneaked Sequoia into the back yard. When we turned to retire, we saw Cindy's little motorcycle tipped forty-five degrees off its rack, but still attached to Hulu. Lesson one, get better tie downs, check frequently.

In the morning we were greeted with Paulina's cheerful *"G'ammy G'ammy"* and Luis loaned me a *Sawzall* to correct some of the consequences of a too low front end. Although we had no plans and no schedule Luis and Megan did, so we left them and headed north to see the Obenski kids. We drove along the coast until it got dark, then discovered how hard it can be to find a place to camp in California, perhaps a vestige of *Grapes of Wrath* days. We pulled into a vacant lot by a railroad track next to some abandoned looking trucks. Within ten minutes we had half the Guadalupe police force banging on our door. "You can't camp in the City of Guadalupe." We did not bother to point out that we, according to their own signs, were outside the city limits. You don't argue with a rude man who has a badge, a gun, attitude and backup.

It turns out they did us an unintentional favor, because the next spot we found was part of Pismo Beach State Park. We pulled in and commandeered the first empty campsite. In the Morning we faced a beautiful view of a huge tree and lagoon. We signed in for the previous night then went for a five mile walk on the beach and saw an orphan baby sea otter. On our way back he was attended by no less than ten rangers and marine mammal experts, wondering why his mother didn't come in for him. It might have been the two surfers that scared her off.

Cindy had never seen Hearst Castle so I insisted we stop there. The nearby San Simeon State park made it easy. It's a shame they call it Hearst Castle. He just called it "the ranch". It's not a castle at all, just a very big house surrounded by four very big guest houses. Not a battlement in sight. What it is, is a museum of a part of W R Hearst's incredibly extensive collection of art and antiquities. It is also a memorial to a very lucky and controversial man who at one time was the largest employer in the US after the Federal government We took two of the four tours one day and a third on the second. The fourth tour was of the gardens, and kind of pointless in October.

Just north of San Simeon we stopped to watch juvenile elephant seals on the beach then drove the legendary coast highway to Monterey. You haven't lived until you do that in a vehicle that's almost nine feet wide. Fortunately, on autumn weekdays there is hardly any traffic.

Monterey has more "No overnight Parking" signs than palm trees, so we got directions to the nearest Camp Wal-Mart. Wal-Mart, unlike many retailers welcomes RVs to use their parking lot overnight, and even has an RV supplies section in the store. They're not naïve; we went in the store and spent almost $100. Next morning, we drove into Salinas to see the very well-done Steinbeck Museum, then on to Santa Cruz to visit Amy and Andy. That's Amy, not Amos. Amy is the soon to be famous singer songwriter in the family.

First interruption, a client in New York needed a report right away, and I learned I can do it without my staff albeit a little crudely. The client was unable to receive it in email form though but partner Jack saved the day by printing it out, editing it and sending a fax and hard copy.

We doubled back to Watsonville to get the front end aligned and confirmed that the air bladder spring for the right front wheel was blown out. This explained the low front end. We made an appointment to get that fixed in Oakland. While we were in Santa Cruz, we introduced UCSC freshman Cory our friend and neighbor in Ocean Beach to UCSC Alumna, Amy. They had great Italian food in SC. Next stop was to visit Ali and Mike in Hayward. Unfortunately, Mike's two kids were with their biological Mom. But my son Steve was able to visit for a mini reunion. Staying at Camp Wal-Mart in Oakland enabled us to be right on time for our service appointment. I tried to take Bohboh out for a little walk, but he climbed under the motor home, on top of the frame and it took two of us to get him out. He ran away from me, right to where Cindy was waiting for him. I went into the store and bought a harness and leash.

The garage valet drove us to the BART station and we were able to go to Alcatraz for the day, while someone else took charge of Hulu. Boh hid under the bed.

I never enjoyed San Francisco until this visit, maybe because I always had to drive or walk. This time we rode in on BART, took a vintage Italian trolley to the pier, and got the last two tickets to Alcatraz. It's a fascinating place, enough so that we bought two books written by former inmates. Most of the visitors the day we were there were not even Americans! The Rangers said they thought being assigned there would be a dead end, but it would not matter, because the novelty would wear off in two or three years and the park would close. Instead, attendance continues to grow even after 20 years. We would have stayed even longer, but we had to get our home out of the shop so we would have a place to sleep.

The narrowest highway passage we encountered was the truck toll lane on I 680. Our mirrors on both sides touched the walls! I don't know what a permit load like a 12' wide mobile home would do.

We were headed for Truckee to meet Uncle Dave, but when Cindy called his cell phone his wife, Mary, answered. It turned out she was returning from a mission of mercy and was essentially right behind us on the freeway. We agreed to a place and met for a delightful dinner, and a chance to get to know Mary one-on-one. She suggested that instead of meeting Dave in Truckee Thursday, we come to their house for the weekend. We camped in the mall parking lot between a bank and a bar. No one seemed to notice us. We got off the freeway and followed some narrow mountain highways toward Portola, the home of the Western Pacific Railway Museum. The highway got so narrow in *Downieville* that we worried about not being able to pass oncoming vehicles or getting trapped on a dead-end street and not being able to turn around. Whoever sat on the right was constantly giving the driver feedback about the edge of the road. Then we came to a one lane bridge, (On a State Highway!) but we did not have to grease the sides to fit through. That happened at the I 680 toll booth to cross the Sacramento River.

When we got to Portola, I reserved a locomotive, then we found a secluded campsite in nearby Tahoe National Forest. National Forest campgrounds are my personal favorites. They have the most private, car accessible campsites. I did not yet have a Golden Age Passport, so we had to pay the full price, $14. The camp host, a Thousand Trails agent, could collect money, but could not sell the Passport. Boh even consented to be walked outdoors, but he slinked like a weasel, ever cautious where there might be a predator bigger than he is.

The Western Pacific Railway Museum is unique. They don't charge admission, instead they rent you a locomotive to drive, and I did. Cindy rode along. It seemed pretty easy, since you don't have to steer, but I noticed the instructor did a lot of things he did not tell me about. Also, I did not have to couple cars, or a hundred other things an engine driver does. It's fun to blow the really BIG horn. The neighbors must hate it. Most diesel locomotives have a long hood and a short hood. It's obvious that the machinery is under the

179

long hood, but what's under the short hood? The engineer's toilet, I hope they stop the train when they use it. The museum had a Union Pacific *Centennial* locomotive open to visitors. I think it's the largest diesel, over 4,000 horsepower on 16 wheels. It's like they put two large locomotives on a common frame.

From there we followed the Western Pacific Railway's Feather River Route over the mountains, to Taylorsville. The route was famous because it was an easier way over the Sierra's than previous railroads. It has a famous 360-degree tunnel where the front of a freight train crosses the rear. We found Taylorsville OK, both buildings. One was closed, while I was inside the saloon asking directions, Dave pulled up behind us so we followed him home instead.

We spent a delightful weekend with them, but decided to leave early on Sunday so Dave and Mary could have some time together without guests. After all guests and fish after three days. By the way although many people offered us their guestrooms, we spent every night on board. We couldn't leave Boh alone. Besides, don't we all sleep better in our own bed? And if you need something in the middle of the night, you know right where it is.

Originally, we thought we would cross the northern tier states, but with winter approaching we decided to keep south, so we went from Maryville through Susanville to…

NEVADA

It's challenging to find the road to Virginia City in the midst of the Reno hooplah, but after three passes we found ourselves on the right narrow byway. Maybe we should have invested in GPS. Halfway up the mountain we stopped at a roadside rest and from it found a beautiful, but abandoned park named after the engineer who built the original road. The park was largely abandoned and it seems mostly used to get drunk and break the bottles.

I had been to Virginia City before and wanted to see it with Cindy. The $3 mining museum was well worth it. In general the less a museum cost the more it had to offer. You pick up funny factoids like: You can't use horses in a mine because if their ears touch the roof, they will rear up and knock themselves out. Mules on the other hand duck. We also walked the whole length of town, on the wooden sidewalks looking at the buildings all most all of which were built right after the 1873 fire. The entire town is a National Historic Place.

It is the site of the Comstock Lode. Named for one of the minor miners, it provided so much silver that Virginia City financed the Civil War, and was also the true source of the Hearst fortune. It is also the reason there is a US mint in nearby Carson City Nevada.

We were looking for a place to camp in Virginia City, and noticed a vacant parking lot. Because of our experience in Guadalupe, we decided to ask a deputy. He said as far as he knew unless a sign said otherwise, we could park for 72 hours. Suddenly a passer-by said he knew someone who camped there for 4 months. In the morning we lugged our computers to a restaurant that offered free Wi-Fi internet. We ordered breakfast and logged on. It was free alright, as but the only sites you could get were the local chamber of commerce, that restaurant and the KOA.

From there we followed US Route 50, the "loneliest road in America" across Nevada. We saw one vehicle heading in the same direction as us for each 100 miles. Then we tried to find a place to camp near Ely. The signs led us to a copper mine. So, we drove into Ruth NV, and asked at a bar. The patrons were friendly and said park anywhere. One even said to park in front of his house and even join his family for breakfast. He neglected to give an address, so we parked in front of what looked like a trailer storage lot. Some of the trailers turned out to be occupied. I took Boh out again, but he did not seem to like it.

We drove the full length of Ely hoping to find lower price for gas. We finally settled for $2.49^9. Then as soon as we left Ely, we entered the Shoshone reservation, where gas was $2.29[9]. And nobody was buying it. A block later we were off the 'res' and gas was back up and the station was busy. This was becoming a pattern. Almost every time we bought gas, it was ten cents cheaper in the next town, or the next day. Gas prices were dropping five cents a day as the mid-term election approached.

We headed south from Ely and stopped for lunch at Cathedral Gorge State Park, Amazing. Nevada wanted $6 to dump a holding tank, the highest price we ever encountered, but the park was spectacular and ought to be better known. The erosion has produced hundreds of multi colored spires, similar to Bryce Canyon, but vertically striated.

We crossed into...

UTAH

At Cedar City and promptly lost the highway. It seems that Rand McNally does not consider a half mile joggle in the state highway significant. There were numerous warning about snow and other hazards on the way from there to Bryce Canyon, but we just proceeded cautiously, and enjoyed the spectacular scenery. We camped at 7000 feet in red Rock Canyon, another National Forest Campsite. I still did not have a Golden Age Passport, so we had to pay the full price, $14. Again, the camp host, a contractor, could collect money, but could not sell the Passport. Needless to say, it got cold that night, 28 degrees. We were concerned about our pipes, but everything was fine.

Next day we drove into Bryce Canyon which I still consider the most gorgeous of our National Parks. There is a tree at Sunrise point that I have seen three times since 1965, and it has grown about an inch. It's still not much bigger than a floor lamp. We hiked down into the canyon at two locations and neither of us had difficulty hiking back up. That night we went to Kodachrome

Basin a Utah State Park and found the campground full. We did get to drive around and admire the colors. Then we asked the ranger where else we might camp. He first suggested KOA, which to us is like a K-mart parking lot, without the ambiance. His next suggestion was to ignore the road closed sign (It's only there so you can't sue the county.) Go 2 miles turn right on a dirt road. Go another mile to a fork, go right then in a half mile find tire tracks off to the right. We did and found ourselves in a hilltop clearing with a spectacular view up into the Bryce Canyon cliffs to the west. I can't figure out why they call it a canyon, since it only has one rim.

We considered continuing on the dirt road to Zion National Park but 40 miles of washboard would be hard on a motorhome, and it might not be passable. We doubled back to Red Rock and continued on the highway to Zion. The west entrance is via a tunnel, actually two consecutive tunnels. Admission was $15, but a Golden Age Passport was $10 and is good for life to enter any Federal recreation site free, and 50% off camping. Let's think carefully before deciding. If I had bought one before we left, it would have paid for itself already. What it did not cover was the $15 escort fee to drive a motorhome through the narrow tunnels. The tunnels are round, except the bottom and the clearance is only 9'11" on the sides, but 13'9" on centerline. So, vehicles over 9'11" must have a one-way tunnel so they can drive right down the middle. We paid the fee, then discovered that due to construction the tunnels were already operating in a one-way mode. *Cest la vie.* The short tunnel is unremarkable, but the one-mile tunnel is unusual in that it has windows! The first time I was in Zion, you were allowed to pull out, park and look out the windows, but traffic has increased and that is no longer possible. Cindy enjoyed the trip down the switchbacks so much that we unloaded her little Honda and rode back up and through the tunnels stopping for photos, and back down. We took the shuttle up the canyon, and took a few hikes. Zion is one of the parks that have gotten too crowded, so they don't allow private cars in the canyon any more. I had to agree the canyon is much more park-like without the traffic.

Cindy wanted to try the Angels Walk, a narrow ridge 2000 feet above the valley with a single rope to hold onto. It's also 4 hours of hiking to get up and back down, so it would have to wait until the next day. Then we got the flash flood warnings.

The campground was full, so we asked a ranger if we could just park in one of the empty parking lots overnight, absolutely not, for the usual bureaucratic reasons. Imagine if Zion NP is the size of this page. The part accessible by road is the size of this sentence! Would it ruin the park to increase the available parking? We were told to try one of the commercial sites in town, or to drive toward LaVerkin. Nothing was available in town, but one ranger had told us that at mile 30 look for lights it the woods. There would be access to BLM land. Sure enough, I recognized the shape of motorhome windows. We forded a little stream and passed a BLM sign warning that this was a flood plain. BLM does not develop campsites, in fact when you are on BLM land it's like you are back in the 19th century. All you have is what you bring. There was however a small enclave of motorhomes. No sooner had we stopped than someone came tapping the driver's side window. He warned us not to turn to the left. He had been stuck there all day, with everyone in the camp helping to get him out.

It rained most of the night. Cindy could not sleep. When I heard someone else leave at 6am I suggested we get out while we could. Carefully backtracking we drove out to the highway. As we made the switch-back at Hurricane, we discovered cell phone service and partook thereof. Contrary to popular belief, you could not get cell phone service everywhere. You are damn lucky to get it anywhere but in town or on the interstate. Steve told me the FCC maps show service for less than 1 percent of the land surface of North America. Of course, 90% of the population lives on that 1%. A lot of the service is provided my marginal suppliers that are not compatible with our phones. During the trip found free Wifi by cruising residential streets with the computer on.

ARIZONA

There are two sides to Grand Canyon Park: the overdeveloped Disneyfied version on the South Rim and the more rustic North Rim. We chose the north rim and were rewarded with winter weather; snow, rain, sleet and hail on the way in. As soon as we checked in to the campground the fog lifted and we walked out to Bright Angel Point where you can look 3000 feet down into the canyon on three sides and Cindy got to experience acrophobia without the 4- hour hike to Angels Landing. We walked along the rim to the visitor center getting a great feel for the canyon. Then the fog closed in. The North Rim facilities were already shutting down and would close for the season the next day. The next morning as we chatted with the rangers a woman asked "What time does the fog go away?" just like it was some scheduled activity. I think I mumbled "April."

As we left, we headed for lower elevation and hopefully warmer weather at Lake Powell. The highway parallels the Vermillion Cliffs and crosses the impressive New Navajo Bridge. The new bridge is cleverly designed to look exactly like its obsolete narrow neighbor but much wider and stronger. The old bridge serves as a pedestrian crossing and canyon viewing platform. A visitor center explains all the environmental considerations that went into the creation of the new bridge, things that presumably were ignored when they built the first one in the old days.

We cruised past Page Arizona and into the Glen Canyon National Recreation Area. I waved my Golden Age Passport at the unattended fee station as we drove by. We checked in for one night and wound-up spending three. This has to be the houseboat capitol of the world. We saw hundreds of them ranging from floating travel trailer to floating 3 story mansions. Lake Powell is 296 miles long with thousands of miles of shoreline. We used the little Honda to go to town and see a movie. We also took the tour of the Glen Canyon Dam (free) and a boat tour of Antelope

Canyon. We skipped the overpriced and tiny Powell Museum. Some people want to remove the dam thinking the canyon would be restored to some former glory. The truth is all that would be exposed would be the bland talus beneath the cliffs, and without the lake, no one would be able to get to the scenery to enjoy it. What is now enjoyed by thousands including the young, old and infirm every summer would be limited to the few hardy souls who can hike the harsh desert, in the spirit of Father Escalante.

Lake Powell was so beautiful we decided that next morning we would try out the folding Porta-Boat we bought when we expected this to be a summer trip. Naturally the next morning the wind was blowing like snot and the clear blue water had turned dark with whitecaps everywhere. We decided to pack up and move on to Four Corners.

On the way we saw the unit train hauling coal to the Navajo power Station, four 6,000 horsepower electric locomotives (The largest ever built) pulling 110 hoppers under a silo to fill them without stopping. Ten thousand tons of coal delivered three times a day. We spent the night at Navajo National Monument. Sign said no RVs over 25 feet, but we had so many sites to choose from we fit just fine. It helps if the rear overhang is long. In spite of the name, the attraction is pre-Navajo cliff dwellings. The Navajo claim ancestry, but some scientists dispute the claim.

Out of curiosity I drove up the road along the 17-mile conveyor that delivers coal to the silo. The belt is only two sections with one break where it angles.

The Four Corners Monument is located on Navajo Land, so the Nation now charges admission. The monument is also surrounded by tacky vender's stalls. The jewelry they sell ranges from good but silly to magnificent. We saw pieces there for $5 similar to what we would later see for $75 in visitor center shops. We walked around the four corners monument, visiting all four states. A woman in the visitor center shanty was demonstrating the art of permanent sand painting, and giving frank answers to questions about trade secrets.

We then drove into…

COLORADO

We actually spent a night in a commercial campground! One with free WIFI that worked.

Rejuvenated everything in Cortez and visited the small but interesting museum.

The next day we went to Mesa Verde NP. This one is a National treasure of pre- Columbian Indian architecture. These structures were abandoned in the twelfth century, and no one knows why. The people left behind food and personal articles, as if they planned to return soon. The workmanship varies, but some of the masonry suggests the mason had a working acquaintance with plumb bobs and levels.

Before taking us down into the canyon the ranger warned us about the elevations, and altitude sickness. It only takes one ranger to take you down, but… Her speech should have disqualified both of us from the hike, but we knew from Bryce and Zion, that we were OK. Boh stayed under the bed. It became apparent from the presentation that these cliff cities were primarily religious centers, not commercial or residential. So they were a small part of a larger civilization.

As we ascended from a second canyon, I challenged two teenage hikers who passed us, "Race you to the top." I fully intended to let them race each other and not try to race with them, but strangely enough when we got up to the mesa, they were behind us.

The park campgrounds were closed for the season, as were the few commercial parks, so rather than backtrack we just parked on top of a hill at a dead end of the frontage road.

Cindy called friends Val and Mike in Denver and we agreed to visit them the next day. Mike gave us specific directions and we drove 370 miles that day crossing the Rockies via Wolf Creek Pass with I think, the only highway the snow shed and Kenosha Pass (10,001 feet) with fresh snow.

Fortunately, the roads were clear and mostly dry. Hulu is computer fuel injected and shrugs off the high altitude without a whimper. Between South Fork and Del Norte, we saw 16 miles of abandoned piggyback rail cars rusting. I pity the people who invested in them as a tax shelter.

We had five friends to see in the Denver area and it turned out they all lived in Lakewood making it super easy. Mike took us to see the Red Rocks amphitheater, a marvelous exploitation of a natural formation. We got to the Buffalo Bill museum just ten minutes to closing time so we ran through and bought the autobiography. BB did more before he was 15 than most people do in a lifetime.

We went downtown exploring with Emily, but found the Molly Brown museum closed.

We walked around and admired the ornate turn of the century churches.

The last day we took the Coors' Brewery tour which was fascinating. Coors controls the entire process from growing their own barley to designing the retail display. The brewery is so large they have their own railroad and export steam to the nearby Colorado School of Mines. This enables the students to brag that they have a pipeline from the brewery to campus.

The tour includes three free beers, then they take you to the gift shop. The T-shirts are much cleverer with half a buzz. I liked Ben Franklin's quotation best "Beer is proof that God loves us and wants us to be happy." Coors leaves tourists with coupons for downtown Golden restaurants then busses them back to their cars parked downtown.

The weather wasn't looking good so we headed south again. We stopped for lunch overlooking the Garden of The Gods. If we were westbound, it would have been colossal, but taken right after the three great canyon National Parks it was just OK. That night we went to La Junta which I remembered from a Boy Scout trip many decades ago. We stopped at the Koshare Kiva Indian Memorial that has an excellent collection of Indian artifacts. A sign in the museum points out that no Native American has ever betrayed the nation he served. Next morning the greeter at Camp Wal-Mart asked if we were ready for the blizzard, the advice was "If you don't get out of Colorado today you won't be getting out for a while.

We headed east, stopping for a few hours at Bent's Old Fort. We were the only guests and had a personal tour. Bent's fort was privately owned and might be best described as a trading post. It was the last US stop on the Santa Fe Trail to Mexico. Nobody knows why, but Bent ultimately burned it down, maybe cholera. What you see today is a restoration. We bought a pair of hand forged scissors in the gift shop for $2 and Cindy says there the best scissors she ever had.

We continued east into...

KANSAS

Expecting little of interest, world's largest ball of string type stuff, first stop was Dodge City, and the Boot Hill Museum. We had it all to ourselves. They have made it very interesting. Starting with the original Boot Hill cemetery they moved or reconstructed all the historic structures onto the same block, so you can see all of it tools, photos, guns, clothing, documents etc., without even going outdoors into the awful Kansas weather. If you want to you can walk all over the new Dodge City and see markers where things happened. Good job.

That night we found a Historic Marker pullout by the highway, with a sign that said "Overnight Parking Permitted – Patrolled by Kansas Highway Patrol" It was remote enough from the highway and coal trains, so we parked there for the night. High winds shook us all night long. In the morning we were surrounded by big rigs and could not leave until they did. On the other hand, they sheltered us from the impending weather.

Before leaving Dodge, we dropped by Old Fort Dodge, which turned out to be an old soldier's home, plus a few mildly historic buildings. That's where we learned that there had been hundreds of tornadoes a few miles to the south.

On our way to the, here it comes, World's Largest Hand Dug Well, we encountered a field of weird metal sculptures, many of which bore an insult to a local politician. There were hundreds, all different, also the world's largest coffee mug collection. A retired farmer (E M) had made one of the sculptures to keep evil spirits or something from scaring his horse. A neighbor complained it was offensive and he replied no it's not, but I'll make one that is. He made more than one, as well as a lot of other things that were cleverly artistic. All with a welder and cutting torch, from junk farm implements, those being more common than sunflowers throughout Kansas.

World's Largest, I can't testify, but the well was huge, 20 feet in diameter and 134 feet deep. There is a steel stairway to the bottom and no we did not pay $3 apiece to descend.

It was dug in the anticipation that the Santa Fe Railway would buy water for the locomotives, but the railroad never came there. The interesting thing was that masons built the casing on top while the miners dug at the bottom. Apparently, there was an iron ring under the stone casing so it could descend as the bottom was dug away.

Medicine lodge was a triple play, three museums for one price. The Medicine Lodge Stockade, where an important treaty was signed with the local Indians, the home of temperance crusader Carry Nation and a two story nineteenth century cabin of questionable renown. We were shown around by the proprietress while we figured out the use on peculiar artifacts. Carry Nation definitely demonstrated how much effect one person can have, good or evil, if they are single minded and persistent.

Independence Kansas has a walking tour of historic homes. Most of these were built during the oil boom of the early 20th century. The tour was interesting, but we had to work around a parade. We asked a student in a band uniform what was going on and he said neo walla, in about the same tone as he might have answered a question as to the day of the week and walked on. Downtown was a huge parade and we heard "neo walla" more than once. To us the highlight of the parade was a father and daughter on a Farmall® tractor painted not Farmall red but Barbie doll pink. We finally cornered a local and asked "What theis neo walla?" Halloween spelled backwards.

One last stop in Kansas, Big Brutus, the largest power shovel still in existence. It's 167 feet high and has an overhead crane inside the house to service the machinery. The bucket holds 90 cubic yards. The visitor center is a nice little museum about surface mining.

That night we took in a movie, and parked overnight without incident outside the theater in Joplin.

MISSOURI

One of my Army buddies said "That's pronounced *Miz'ery.*" From Joplin we went to the George Washington Carver National Monument. He was quite a guy. Both Henry Ford and Thomas Edison offered him huge sums of money to work for them, but he stayed at Tuskegee and worked for (and on) peanuts. He sent his students into industry. He was the one who gave Ford the idea to build plastic car bodies from soy beans.

We took a short dogleg to the southernmost corner of Missouri to visit the Cliff Dwellers Cave, as this one cave offered almost everything to be seen in a cave and was nearby. It was a family run affair and did not take too much. I'm not much of a cave guy. On the highway to the cave the signs said low clearance, 11'5" and we thought we might have to unload the bike to ride the final miles. It tuned out the low clearance was an overhang that only affected one lane so we were able to bypass it by driving in the wrong lane a short distance. The cave met our expectations, no more, no less.

We set out to cross Missouri on secondary roads, but the narrow twisting nature beat us into submission. We quickly tired of the view of oak trees and run-down trailer houses. We got on the interstate. A tour of America's only remaining barrel factory got our attention, but due to a fire in the gift shop it was closed. We next tried to find the Daniel Boone Grave/Memorial, which took a lot of backtracking to reveal almost nothing, just a stone on a hill. Then to his final home which was hidden down 20 miles of narrow back roads. We got there just in time for the last short tour of the day. It's amazing how many of our icon individuals were lawyers back when the law fit in one book. His home was built like a small fort since the Indians were not completely subdued.

We found our way back to the real roads, but what we could not find was a campground. Finally, out of desperation Cindy asked a Deputy Sherriff, who sent us to a park and ride that turned out to be reasonably quiet.

We drove into Hannibal on the "Business Route". It led into the most run-down area I had seen in 20 years, but with persistence we found the real downtown and the Mark Twain Museum. This was cleverly done connecting half-a-dozen buildings that linked to the man, his stories, and his real life. The town also had a lot of tourist businesses that exploited the connection with no real link.

From Hannibal we drove to Wapelo, Iowa, where we quickly located Cindy's Uncle Gene at a C-store. We stopped at Old Fort Madison, on the way, but found it closed for the season. Gene set us up at a hookup in the County Fairgrounds and took us home to Aunt Lois. Next day Lois had to work, but Gene took us around and introduced us to everyone in Louisa County, living or dead. When we went to pay for the campsite, we were told that Gene had prepaid. Then I discovered that I had dropped the wrong envelope into the iron ranger. We had to go to city hall to straighten out the problem. The clerk offered to go get the envelope for me. Just to be nice I said if she would trust me with the key, I would go get it, so she did! When I brought the key back, she tried to give back my fee money, but I told her to put it in the cookie fund.

The weather was not to our liking, so we kept moving, this time on to Moline to try to find the John Deere Pavilion. It was a bit of a challenge because the streets in Rock Island and Moline have the same confusing numbering plan, but not the same numbers.

Avenues and streets are both numbered, but are at right angles so it's possible to be at third and third or fiftieth and fiftieth, in two different places. We eventually found what I thought would be a museum or visitor center, and it was, but it was more like a dealer showroom too. John Deere had learned to sell $250,000 combines the same way Harley Davidson sold $6,000 motorcycles. Brand, brand, brand, they have tchotchkes of every description from key rings to T-shirts to mailboxes to toys to furniture with the brand, all in "John Deere Green".

I wanted to see the Rock Island Arsenal Museum. Cindy was tired so I was left on my own. They had the most amazing collection of small arms imaginable; I would estimate 5,000 weapons everything ever carried by an American Soldier or fired at one since the Civil War. The Arsenal had made over the years just about anything the Army needed from a spoon to a cannon. Outside, they had an equally impressive collection of crew-served weapons, from a mountain howitzer to a Sherman tank.

Being this far north had major disadvantages. Our refrigerator kept going out, and campgrounds, if they were not completely closed and chained off, had the water turned off. Twice we had to beg for a connect to a hydrant to refill our water. We learned that Flying J truck stops had every fluid an RV could need and allowed overnight parking.

We continued a little further north to visit Cindy's Aunt IlEileen and Uncle Bob, then plunged south toward Springfield. Wheels of Time Museum, sounded interesting, but it was closed for the season. We stopped at the Lincoln Courtroom Museum in Beardstown; the museum based on the only courtroom in which Lincoln had practiced that is still in service(once a month). They have however built a passable museum around it and we got another personal tour.

We drove to Springfield (IL only has one Springfield) to see the Lincoln Library and Museum, but the next morning at Oh dark hundred we got the fateful call. Cindy's Dad had suddenly taken a turn for the worse and was not expected to make it. I called Southwest Airlines, since they fly frequently and nearly everywhere. That night we were in San Diego Mercy Hospital at Don's bedside hoping he would live. Two family members allowed in the room at a time. The rest of the family commandeered an entire waiting room. Next morning, he was a little bit better! Daughters flew in from all over the country. Slowly he was recovering. I returned to St. Louis to feed the cat and Cindy returned the next day. (Don recovered and had a couple more good years after his two-month ordeal.)

On the plane back to St. Louis…

MISSOURI

…Cindy learned that there was a very special showing of Chihuly blown glass at the Missouri Botanical Garden. The glassware was mixed into the botanical displays in a delightful tease, enhancing both. The gardens were more interesting than most because many of the plant tags had a short anecdote about the species instead of just an unpronounceable Latin name. Being back in St. Louis we took a look at the Gateway Arch and Eads' Bridge, then crossed back into…

ILLINOIS

…to see the world's largest Catsup (Not ketchup) bottle. It's a factory water tower. Back to Springfield. The Lincoln Library Museum is as with most things about Lincoln impressive, humbling and emotional. The technology is also amazing. Put this on your must-see list.

So many things were closed that we decided to accelerate the northern portion of our travels. We highballed across the rest of Illinois and all of Indiana until we got to Dayton...

OHIO

...and the Air Force Museum. We spent an hour driving in a huge circle trying to find it. We got there just two hours to closing. There are six building, each the size of a football field. Each dedicated to an era in the development of military flying. The buildings are so large a B29 seems ordinary and even the B52 bombers (2 of them) seem like just another airplane. I give the Air Force credit for displaying their mistakes along with their triumphs, and their enemy's triumphs alongside their own.

A nostalgic side trip to Barberton to see what's left of the B&W plant where I worked. Many of the old buildings are gone and what's left appears to be the sterile new ones.

Areas that used to be quiet country roads have been overwhelmed by suburban shopping malls, but the house I remodeled in Uniontown has been further improved and looks quaint.

PENNSYLVANIA

...via the Turnpike we bypassed Pittsburgh, then left it for the old highways. Fog closed in and when I saw a sign that said camping, I turned in. It turned out to be a fishing camp and closed for the season. I shoved ten bucks in the slot and found a place to park for a stormy night. Next morning, we drove to the Allegheny Portage Railroad Museum. Back when canals were the latest way to travel, The Erie Canal was drawing all the traffic away from

Pennsylvania because it took 23 days to get from Philadelphia to Pittsburgh. Most of that time was a difficult wagon ride over Allegheny Mountain. The portage railroad hauled canal barges over the mountain using stationary steam engines and, at first, horses on the level part. Barges could be separated into segments, the first inter-modal containers.

Seven miles away we visited the Horseshoe Curve of the Pennsylvania Railroad. That refinement put the portage railroad out of business and is still one of the most heavily used railroad sections in the world. The Horseshoe Curve Museum tickets were good for the Railroad Employees Memorial Museum in Altoona so we went to that. Once again, we had a museum virtually to ourselves. This one was focused on the people of the Pennsy, and the railroad culture. The railroad was run scientifically and everything was analyzed from the best type of coal to burn down to the brooms used to sweep up the coaches.

You can never go home. I went back to the Penn State Campus and could barely find it. The town had changed so much. We followed 180 through the rural parts of eastern PA where the bears are said to outnumber the people to get to Steamtown® National Monument in Scranton. We arrived on a weekday off season when the locomotives are not fired up. We had it to ourselves. Steamtown was built around the culture of the Delaware, Lackawanna and Western, a line that prided itself on the relative cleanliness of its anthracite fired locomotives.

From Scranton we headed south to meet my brother Mike and his wife Tina. Mike owned the biggest cat house in PA; he's a veterinarian. We enjoyed three days with them, catching up and comparing notes, recommending things to see. Tried to show Cindy the Quakertown Mart, which is unlike anything in the west, a mile long indoor farmers flea market, but once again, wrong day of the week. We went to Doylestown looking for the Mercer Museum, found the Mercer House and Pottery works instead. Frederick Mercer was somewhat of an eccentric visionary. In 1910, he built his huge house out of concrete using only unskilled labor, so the workers would do everything his way. Re-bar had not been invented yet. Like Hearst he favored concrete for its total fire resistance. In his case he had personal experience from being trapped in a burning barn. The tickets to the house included along with a personal tour, directions to the museum. Threading an RV through the pre revolution streets of Doylestown convinced me to leave Philadelphia off the itinerary.

The Museum, like the house was built entirely of concrete. A modern elevator takes one to the top and the tour is a descent. Mercer was concerned that the industrial revolution would wipe out centuries of knowledge of skilled tradesmen so he collected the tools of each trade. Each trade has a room or gallery in the museum. The butcher, the baker, the blacksmith, the farrier, the whaler, dozens of collections gleaned from estate sales show multiple examples of the tools used by 18th and 19th century artisans to provide for their needs and the needs of their customers. The ingenuity of people who had to make do or do without is uncanny. Bought more books.

We drove through my hometown of Hatboro at night looking for a Wal-Mart, that turned out to be closed, but we parked in the lot overnight. In the morning we drove past my high school, which has not changed, and went to Neshaminy Creek where my family used to play. It's now a huge but sterile State Park.

Once again, we headed south racing winter. Plunged through Philly and Wilmington…

DELAWARE

…on I95 then took off on a gray map line to quaint Delaware City and had lunch on the banks of the river with the same name. We crossed the C&D canal on a short high narrow bridge to the Delmarva Peninsula, also known as the Eastern Shore, and historically as the "Land of Pleasant Living". This rural area was once the main source of protein in the form of poultry and seafood to the big cities. Assembly line housing seems to be taking over.

We quickly found ourselves in…

MARYLAND

…and perhaps the worst designed freeway rest area in America. To save money the rest area was located in the median so it could serve both directions. It had nice long deceleration lanes for getting in, but no acceleration lane to get out. Instead, it was necessary to make a sharp left turn into the crowded fast lane. What were they thinking?

Gasoline competition seemed limited it was almost all $2.17^9 per gallon, but I found a station at $2.07^9 so I filled up, but it was 10% ethanol, and I suspect 9% water. Ethanol has only 60% of the energy of gasoline so it was as if each gallon was only 96% gas and 4% air 96% of 2.179 is 2.092, so it was not as much a bargain as it looked, unless the other gas was also diluted. We crossed another high, narrow, but 4-mile-long bridge across the Chesapeake Bay into Annapolis. This explains the name of the C&D canal if you didn't get it. We met up with my college neighbor and sailing buddy Terry who showed us around the city and local curiosities.

We moved on from there to Silver Spring and met Cindy's niece Courtney. Courtney drove us to Frederick MD to visit the museum of Civil War Medicine. It is small but well designed and totally changes one's beliefs about the state of medical knowledge at the time. It can be fascinating, but it's definitely not for everyone. Next day Courtney went to work and we went took the Metro to the Holocaust Museum. We were there when they opened the doors and only because they stayed open late for a special event were, we not ejected at closing time. It is something everyone should experience. Even though the Holocaust is over genocide is still with us, recently in Darfur, and Somalia. In the 20th century over 100 million people were slaughtered by their own governments.

We tried to go to the movies that night, but on top of that museum, comedy just did not work. Next morning, we moved to an RV park where we could hook up and recharge, then took the metro again, this time to the Spy Museum. This one is really fascinating both at the technology level and the human boldness and ingenuity level. Spying (intelligence in military speak) changes the outcome of war as much as weapons, logistics or training. More importantly it sometimes enables a nation to avoid a war, or a battle, altogether.

VIRGINIA

We allowed the calendar to intrude just a little and drove on to celebrate Thanksgiving at Deanna and Ron's in Herndon.

Cindy showed Dianna her prize-winning turkey technique and we all gorged on the usual assortment of holiday decadence, while we discussed possible remedies for the destruction being done by the local beavers. When I called my girls to commemorate the Holiday, I learned that my son Steve was in DC, so we arranged to meet him in Alexandria where Cindy surprised him with a tiny turkey baked in the 5-inch-high RV oven. We had to measure every small turkey in the market and finally found one that was squashed to the necessary dimension.

We found a National Park campground that was open, but without services. Virginia road signs drove us nuts. Every road seemed to have a number, but they reused the numbers. Signs had too many words and were too close to the decision point for modern speeds, sometimes right in the gore between two ramps.

In spite of the confusion, we were able to find Monticello. It was late so we decided to put it off until morning. Charlottesville had the only Walmart we had seen so far with no overnight RV parking, but we found a movie theater and after watching a movie spent the night in a lot they shared with a gym.

Monticello is an interesting study in the man and the lifestyle of a Southern Planter. Although we all admire Jefferson it is difficult to reconcile his extravagant lifestyle with the privation of his slaves. It's true he died broke, but that was because he spent all his money. His wife died after only ten years of marriage, having given birth to four children. Many people attributed her death to the rigors of four pregnancies in ten years. This did not impress Cindy who had six. That Monticello is preserved is a tribute to the Levy family that bought it, maintained it and donated it to an historical trust.

Close to Monticello is Ash Lawn, Highland the more humble home of James Monroe, a stark contrast about halfway between Monticello and the typical family farm.

From Charlottesville we tried to take the Blue Ridge Parkway, but found sections of it closed in anticipation of bad weather that never developed. We spent so much time on detours that in one 24-hour period we made good only 40 miles. We came across the cabin memorial of a rural woman who after giving birth to 24 children, none of whom survived infancy became a midwife and delivered 295 other babies successfully. She never lost a baby or a mother. We managed to drive most of the Blue Ridge in installments between closed sections and accidentally found a fascinating free geology museum. On the other hand, $12 apiece to see the VA Natural Bridge struck us as exorbitant.

NORTH CAROLINA

We had Cindy's Cousin Sherry and her husband for dinner in Hulu, in Asheville in a Sears parking lot. This odd arrangement was necessitated by their downtown residence where parking would be impossible. Rent-a-cop Barney Fife insisted we not spend the night, but gave us good directions to Camp Wal-Mart. It was cute the way he wore his immaculate uniform and took his job so seriously.

We found our way back onto the Blue Ridge and used it to enter Great Smokies NP. First of all, the smoky condition predates Columbus, can't blame whitey for this one. The scenery is as spectacular as the west, but mostly green instead of bare rock. The park has preserved many antebellum structures, including entire pioneer farms, the kind that made-do without slaves. It is always fascinating to see the ingenuity of isolated people.

The western entrance to the park is via Gatlinburg...

TENNESSEE

...The southern Baptist version of Las Vegas is every bit as outrageous, tacky and overdone without the pervasion of gambling or overt sex. We plunged deep into Tennessee drawn by two magnets, The American Museum of Science and Energy at Oak Ridge and the Jack Daniels Distillery tour. We found a place to camp at the Old Stone Fort State Park. We were the only campers there. The Ranger came around at 8:30 to collect a few dollars and advise us that it would be 19 degrees by morning and snow was on the way. Then he admonished us to see the "Fort" which was really the mile and a half long remnant of a wall surrounding what is thought to be a 2,000-year-old ceremonial ground, not fort. Next morning, to keep warm, we ran around the perimeter which was so worn down as to be almost indistinguishable from a natural formation. The visitor center however had an excellent time line display.

The American Museum of Science and Energy did not seem to qualify as American, more like perhaps Tennessee, but it had some good points and some good interactive items for the students we did not have with us. The fun part was Grossology, all about bodily fluids. That was at least worth the price of admission. The Jack Daniels tour however was a disappointment. I'll attribute it to the smug attitude of the guide we got and let it go.

We bored our way south. Nothing looked promising in…

ALABAMA

…We just crashed right through to…

FLORIDA

Landed at Fort Walton Beach where the sand looks and feels like refined sugar. The water was almost warm enough, almost. We drove west along the Gulf coast. You cannot help but notice the empty lots where a hurricane removed buildings, right down to the footers, and the new colossal hotels and condos going. All the smaller buildings on the Gulf coast are either patched up, boarded up or brand new. Where the highway turns inland a little in Mobile Bay (oops, that's…

ALABAMA

…again) there are some genteel older structures. Then you get to…

MISSISSIPPI

…and more of the same Hurricane aftermath.

LOUISIANA

It seems like most of Louisiana is under water. We crossed a very long bridge across Lake Pontchartrain to get to New Orleans and it's disturbing. Big box stores like Target and Wal-Mart were still boarded up because there are no customers. Downtown office buildings are boarded up because there is no business. The only thing that appeared back to normal was Harrah's. Houses, entire neighborhoods, like a biblical injunction, were marked for demolition. FEMA trailer houses four abreast stretched for miles. We had to escape across another long bridge over Lake Pontchartrain. Louisiana was too depressing and we just made a bee line for Texas. Passing through Lake Charles and its chemical plants, Cindy was overcome and almost passed out. Fortunately, some fresh…

TEXAS

…air seemed to revive her in about an hour, although some symptoms persisted for the remainder of the trip.

Texas has the largest visitor center we saw. They divide the State into 5 regions and those are bigger than most states. I asked our favorite question. "What if someone only had time for one thing in Texas, where would you send him?"

"That wouldn't be fair to the other places."

"OK what do you have in Texas that they don't have anywhere else?"

"The Alamo."

"No, that may be special to Texan's, but it's just another Spanish Mission to us.

California has one on every corner." "There is the Texas Museum." "Nahhhh."

But I found it on my own. The Ocean Star, an offshore oil platform museum. A real production platform jacked up in Galveston Harbor and made into a museum.

We also found a darling little Edison Museum in Port Arthur where they were unloading 100-foot-long windmill blades. We had a hard time leaving Port Arthur though, because a huge refinery tower was being moved along the main highway at ½ mile per hour.

We got to the Texas Gulf coast and found more of the same hurricane aftermath, with one difference, Texas water is brown from the silt beaches. We spent our first Texas night at Fort Morgan overlooking Galveston Harbor. The ranger gave us the combination to the gate, in case we had to go out and left the whole park to us.

Next morning, we went to the Ocean Star. We happened in on it the day the new Schlumberger customer service hires were on a tour. I learned more about oil in an hour than a three-credit class. We continued down the Texas coast, hoping to make it to Corpus Christy, when in Port La Vaca we got word of another storm. The water was still looking brown, so we headed inland to see friends and relatives in San Antonio. Now Florida appears to be the flattest state, since the high point is 345 ft. But Texas has enough land within 50 feet of sea level to make three of Florida, and that gets boring. Another thing about Texas, you never arrive. All the mileages have three digits.

Well, we had to go through San Antonio and it was too early to see anyone, so we visited the Alamo. It's right downtown, so parking was a bit of a challenge. There was plenty of it, but they wanted $10 for cars and $50 for an RV. I took 2 on street spaces and put $20 in the slot. It's a nice mission, but it's only a shrine if you're a Texan.

We visited a bit, got lost a lot and headed for Austin. My old friend Jack describes Austin as the blueberry in tomato soup. It was apparently the only place in Texas that did not worship *dubbya*. We spent three days with Jack and Lydia rediscovering why Jack and I had been such good friends in the Army especially in the isolation of the Bar XC days.

Then we headed west. This is when you really understand Texas. From any other city in Texas to El Paso it's five hundred miles! There is nothing in between. I was beginning to worry, because Hulu's gas mileage dropped to about 6, but it must have been the gas I got outside Austin because it improved with each subsequent thankful. Excess ethanol I suspect.

NEW MEXICO

We were beginning to get close to our time limit, so we just drove right past the souvenir shops that seem to be the only thing in southern New Mexico and pressed on into…

ARIZONA

We skipped "The Thing" (another souvenir shop) and turned right at Tucson, following the scenic route to Globe, which like State College had grown beyond recognition. Rather than double back on US 60 to Phoenix, Cindy charted a course on AZ 88 past Roosevelt Dam. Although I had worked in the area for a year, I had never been past the dam. AZ 88 was built to be able to build the dam, and although it's a state highway it is unpaved. It's also so narrow that people kept stopping us to warn about it. The scenery is spectacular. It's as if you were allowed to drive through the Grand Canyon. It was well worth every bump and narrow defile.

We stopped to spend a few days with Kim and Beth in Gilbert near Phoenix. The riparian reserve in Gilbert is a wonderful asset, but the rest of Sun Valley leaves me wanting to escape. Like LA and Las Vegas, the suburbs go on endlessly. I think of Phoenix as 100,000 strip malls in search of a city.

From Phoenix we made a virtual nonstop run for SAN DIEGO and a daughters graduation from lawschool.

OTHER BOOKS BY KENNETH (KEN) S. OBENSKI

Forensic Engineering Reconstruction of Accidents,
With John Fiske Brown, Charles C. Thomas
Publishing, 1990, 254pp

Motorcycle Accident Reconstruction, Understanding
Motorcycles Lawyers and Judges Publishing, 1994,
223pp

Motorcycle Accident Reconstruction and Litigation,
With Paul F. Hill Lawyers and Judges Publishing,
1997, 1130pp

Expert Witness Confessions, As Kyle Spectator,
iUniverse, 2007, 142pp

Motorcycles, So You Think You Want To Ride,
Lawyers and Judges Publishing, 2014, 56pp

He also writes a biweekly column for West Hawaii
Today Newspaper

Lightning Source UK Ltd.
Milton Keynes UK
UKHW041223050821
388337UK00001B/31